Applying Dynamic Assessment in Schools

from the author

Improving Learning Through Dynamic Assessment
A Practical Classroom Resource
Fraser Lauchlan and Donna Carrigan
ISBN 978 1 84905 373 0
eISBN 978 0 85700 731 5

of related interest

Getting More Out of Restorative Practice in Schools
Practical Approaches to Improve School Wellbeing and Strengthen Community Engagement
Edited by Margaret Throsborne, Nancy Riestenberg and Gillean McCluskey
Foreword by Fania E. Davis
ISBN 978 1 78592 776 8
eISBN 978 1 78450 692 6

For Flourishing's Sake
Using Positive Education to Support Character Development and Wellbeing
Frederika Roberts
Foreword by Andrew Cowley
ISBN 978 1 78775 024 1
eISBN 978 1 78775 025 8

APPLYING DYNAMIC ASSESSMENT IN SCHOOLS

A Practical Approach to Improve Learning

Fraser Lauchlan
and
Clare Jones Daly

Illustrated by Masha Pimas

Jessica Kingsley Publishers
London and Philadelphia

First published in Great Britain in 2023 by Jessica Kingsley Publishers
An imprint of John Murray Press

1

Copyright © Fraser Lauchlan and Clare Jones Daly 2023

The right of Fraser Lauchlan and Clare Jones Daly to be identified as the Author of the Work has been asserted by them in accordance with the Copyright, Designs and Patents Act 1988.

Front cover image source: Masha Pimas

All rights reserved. No part of this publication may be reproduced, stored in a retrieval system, or transmitted, in any form or by any means without the prior written permission of the publisher, nor be otherwise circulated in any form of binding or cover other than that in which it is published and without a similar condition being imposed on the subsequent purchaser.

All pages marked ✳ may be photocopied and downloaded for personal use with this programme, but may not be reproduced for any other purposes without the permission of the publisher.

A CIP catalogue record for this title is available from the British Library and the Library of Congress

ISBN 978 1 83997 338 3
eISBN 978 1 83997 339 0

Printed and bound in Great Britain by Bell & Bain Limited

Jessica Kingsley Publishers' policy is to use papers that are natural, renewable and recyclable products and made from wood grown in sustainable forests. The logging and manufacturing processes are expected to conform to the environmental regulations of the country of origin.

Jessica Kingsley Publishers
Carmelite House
50 Victoria Embankment
London EC4Y 0DZ

www.jkp.com

John Murray Press
Part of Hodder & Stoughton Limited
An Hachette UK Company

FSC
www.fsc.org
MIX
Paper | Supporting responsible forestry
FSC® C007785

INTRODUCTION

This textbook is intended to introduce the reader to a contemporary approach to dynamic assessment and intervention work. It is targeted to all those working in education who may already have some knowledge about the approach, as well as those who may know nothing about it. This will include educational psychologists, speech and language therapists, special educational needs coordinators (SENCOs), classroom teachers, learning support teachers, teaching assistants, and many others. It may also be helpful for parents who work closely with their children at home. The book will outline the various concepts underlying the dynamic assessment approach, make links between theory and practice explicit, and offer some practical resources that can have a direct impact on improving a child's learning in the classroom setting, and also in how they learn at home.

How does dynamic assessment improve learning? As we will discuss below, dynamic assessment uses an interactive approach in order to identify those cognitive and emotional aspects of learning that are in the process of developing but are not fully developed, and thus targets these areas for intervention in the classroom, or even at home. The use of mediated learning skills (as described below) can foster further development of these identified cognitive and emotional aspects of learning. It is the intention of this book to help practitioners in implementing the practical elements of dynamic assessment accordingly.

What is contained in this book?

In Chapter 1, we outline the key elements of the dynamic assessment approach, briefly describe the work of Lev Vygotsky, whose ideas have had the single biggest impact on the development of the approach, and we introduce the model of the Dynamic Triad of Effective Learning. We underline the distinction that is made between dynamic assessment as administered by researchers, and dynamic assessment as implemented by practitioners. It is the latter that is a focus of this book. In Chapter 1, we also introduce our contemporary approach to dynamic assessment, and by this we mean a more flexible interpretation of the ideas and concepts in order to extend the possibilities for helping children and young people with their learning in a range of contexts, and utilizing a range of educational personnel, rather than restricting the possibilities to one-to-one traditional assessment work.

In Chapter 2, we focus on what mediated learning is, and how, as practitioners, we can develop our mediated learning skills and use them more effectively in our assessment and intervention work with children and young people. In addition to mediated learning, a key aspect of dynamic assessment is the identification of Cognitive and Affective Learning

Principles. These are the aspects of the child's learning that can be observed when working on a given task. By identifying those aspects of learning that require specialized intervention, perhaps those that are in the process of developing, but are not yet fully developed, educators can work towards setting realizable goals and implement a cohesive and coordinated plan of intervention.

In Chapter 3, we describe these Cognitive and Affective Learning Principles and outline how talking about them with the children themselves, using our child-friendly resources, can be a valuable way forward for making positive changes in the classroom. Depending on the age and stage of the child, dynamic assessment can help the child be more aware of what they could do to enhance their learning as they are fully involved in the process. We have designed materials with child-friendly language and visual aids that can assist the child in understanding their learning style (see Chapters 3 and 7).

Chapter 4 describes the tasks and materials that you can use when doing dynamic assessment. While we recognize that there are specially designed materials for dynamic assessment available, which we will briefly discuss, not having these materials should not deter you from engaging with the process. We believe that dynamic assessment can be done with any games or activities that involve thinking processes and problem solving. Some suggestions for suitable tasks and materials are described in this chapter.

Chapter 5 focuses on the feeding-back process of dynamic assessment – or as we prefer to call it, feeding forward. This part is crucial for making sure there is a positive outcome from the dynamic assessment. There are various ways in which this can be done, and we will discuss these in this chapter, including how you can incorporate goal theory into your feeding-forward process.

Chapter 6 outlines the concept of the Dynamic School, which is a method that can be adopted to work towards a whole-school ethos change.

Chapter 7 has all the photocopiable/downloadable resources and worksheets referred to in the previous chapters.

> All resources marked with ✳ are photocopiable and can also be downloaded from https://library.jkp.com/redeem using the code UWXGPLG. Here you can also access supplementary material containing the following: 1) Effective assessment: the swim race analogy, 2) Creating dynamic learners: upskilling the future ready workforce (a focus on developing innovation and entrepreneurship) and 3) Spotlight on practice: working with bilingual, multilingual and EAL children.

Contents

Acknowledgements 7

Introduction 9

Part 1: Fundamentals of Dynamic Assessment

1. An Introduction to Dynamic Assessment 13

2. Mediated Learning 17

3. Cognitive and Affective Learning Principles 29

4. Dynamic Assessment Materials 41

5. Feedforward 47

Part 2: The Dynamic School and Practical Resources

6. The Dynamic School 55

7. Resources 69

References 175

Subject Index 179

Author Index 183

Acknowledgements

Our dynamic assessment journey has been enriched by a vast community of inspirational people, including children and young people who have helped us define and develop our ideas, all the dynamic assessment practitioners who have participated in our workshops, Donna Carrigan for allowing us to reference and further develop some of the ideas from her work with Fraser (*Improving Learning Through Dynamic Assessment*, 2013) in this book, and the wonderful staff at Thornlie Primary School for being the first to embrace and promote dynamic assessment practices across their whole school.

We are also grateful for the guidance and support we have personally received from the following in our quest to develop potential: Professor Jim Boyle, Dr Elizabeth King MBE and Dr Phil Stringer.

We would like to thank our long-suffering families who are regularly subjected to our ideas and innovations, but who put up with them willingly, and even contribute to their development with curiosity and enthusiasm; they are the epitome of being dynamic.

Finally, we would like to thank you for reading this book and joining us on our dynamic assessment journey. Join our network of inspiring people by visiting our website www.dynamicassessmentuk.com.

Part 1

Fundamentals of Dynamic Assessment

CHAPTER 1

AN INTRODUCTION TO DYNAMIC ASSESSMENT

Background

In 2013, the first author's previous book (with Donna Carrigan), *Improving Learning Through Dynamic Assessment: A Practical Classroom Resource*, was published. In the intervening ten years, the way in which children and young people learn has changed significantly. Some of this is down to a natural process of change and development, but since March 2020, as a result of the Covid-19 pandemic, children and young people have been faced with dramatic changes in how they learn, and teachers and educators have had to learn new methods in which to impart that learning. Online platforms, virtual lessons and google meets have become the norm. However, children and young people are still being assessed by the same traditional methods which take little or no account of their acquired skills and potential. Learning has had to adapt. Assessment also has to adapt. One technique that can capture this adapted learning and provide a valuable framework for improving learning is dynamic assessment.

Dynamic assessment is an interactive assessment and intervention process. Based on the theories of Vygotsky (1978), dynamic assessment helps those working with learners to identify constructs that the learner:

- has already mastered (*Zone of Actual Development*)
- is currently trying to understand or tasks they can do with scaffolding (*Zone of Proximal Development*)
- is unable to do yet independently (*Zone of Potential Development*).

This is achieved by the assessor or instructor implementing mediated learning skills to scaffold the child's learning and unleash their potential. The dynamic assessment approach offers an alternative means of assessing children, which has until now been used mostly by educational psychologists and speech therapists but is being increasingly recognized by all those working in education. Dynamic assessment is based on the notion that you can learn more about a child's cognitive development by working with them in a collaborative way, rather than merely assessing what they can do on their own (Vygotsky, 1978). The collaborative aspect of the assessment context, as well as a more flexible approach to how the assessment is administered (to explore a child's learning style), are key characteristics of dynamic assessment (see below for more detail).

In contrast to standardized methods of assessment, the aim of dynamic assessment is not to compare a standardized score with the norm of an age group, but instead to explore *how* a child learns, and *which aspects* of their learning require intervention. The focus is on the adult-child relationship based on the theory of mediated learning, and how this can help the child improve aspects of their learning. The concept of mediated learning is a core feature of dynamic assessment.

Mediated learning is just one aspect of dynamic assessment and will be examined in more detail in Chapter 2. Figure 1.1 outlines the Dynamic Triad of Effective Learning where there are three elements that constitute dynamic assessment: mediated learning, Cognitive and Affective Learning Principles, and finally, the task or content used to work with a child.

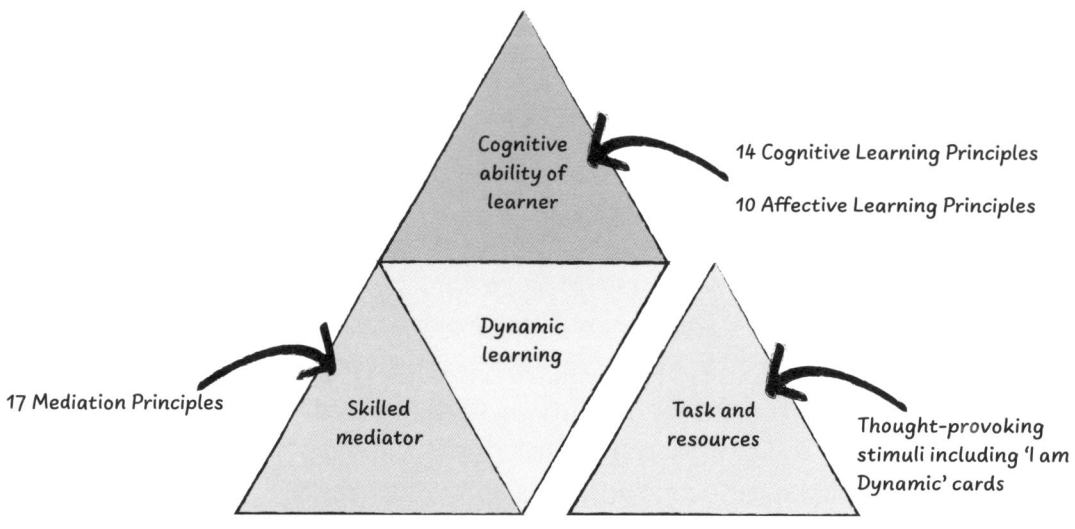

Figure 1.1: The Dynamic Triad of Effective Learning

Dynamic assessment for practitioners

Before we go any further it is important to acknowledge the lack of consensus regarding the definition of dynamic assessment. As Stringer (2018) has highlighted, the number of definitions of dynamic assessment has multiplied in recent years, and it is fair to say that the approach, and its associated concepts, is being used in various contexts, and in various professions. (For some examples, see Bosma, Stevenson & Resing, 2017 (working with children with arithmetic difficulties); Camilleri, Hasson & Dodd, 2014 (working with bilingual children); Hasson & Joffe, 2007 (speech and language therapy); Hessels, Vanderlinden & Rojas, 2011 (research on eye movement); and Merghati & Ahangari, 2015 (working with EFL learners).)

We would argue that despite the multitude of approaches to dynamic assessment, and its application in a myriad of contexts and professions, there are still three core features that make it distinguishable compared to other approaches, namely:

1. There is a collaborative nature to the assessment context, based on the Vygotskian notion that we can learn just as much, if not more, about a child's cognitive development, and how they learn, by working with them, together, rather than assessing what they can do on their own.
2. There is a flexible nature to the assessment, whereby we do not need to stick to rigid procedures or scripts. As assessors, if we wish to take a different direction during the

assessment because we think it will be more productive in terms of exploring the child's learning, then we will.
3. There is a focus on emerging cognitive skills (processes) rather than those that are fully developed (products), as well as a focus on the affective or emotional factors of learning.

The dynamic assessment approach we describe in this textbook adheres to these three elements and they form the basis for the application of the approach in practical settings. Our resources and ideas have been developed over a combined period of 40 years of practical experience of using dynamic assessment in our work as educational psychologists (Lauchlan, 2001, 2012, 2013; Lauchlan & Carrigan, 2013; Lauchlan, Carrigan & Daly, 2007; Lauchlan & Elliott, 1997, 2001).

Elliott (2003) and others (Kozulin, 2011; Poehner & Lantolf, 2005; Tzuriel, 2011) have made an important distinction between dynamic assessment that is *done by researchers* and that which is *done by practitioners*. The former is largely quantitative, more often than not involving a scoring of a child's performance with and without assistance and may involve an attempt to measure 'learning potential' (see Grigorenko, 2009; Guthke, Beckmann & Dobat, 1997; Hessels, 2000; Naglieri, 2000; and Tzuriel, 2011 for further discussion and examples). However, the inherent problems there are with trying to measure the construct of learning potential have been noted by Frisby and Braden (1992), Lidz (2014) and Stringer (2018). Lidz (2014) argued that, over time, she became increasingly less interested in the idea of measuring learning potential since 'we all have potential beyond our current level of functioning' (p.301), therefore the construct becomes largely meaningless.

Dynamic assessment that is done by practitioners, including educational psychologists, tends to be largely qualitative, involving the accumulation of qualitative information regarding the child's learning, which would then form the basis of feedback to the child's parents and classroom teacher in an attempt to effect positive change in the classroom. It is the qualitative approach, targeted by dynamic assessment practitioners, that we outline in this textbook. By practitioners we mean mainly educational psychologists, but also speech and language therapists, learning support teachers, teachers, teaching assistants, and all others working in education. Some of the ideas of dynamic assessment may also be valuable for parents who want to help their children at home, particularly those who focus on mediated learning.

It is our view is that it is more valuable for practitioners to take a much wider view of what dynamic assessment can be, and how the ideas associated with the approach can be adapted. While we acknowledge that the traditional notion of dynamic assessment is where an assessor (usually an educational psychologist) works one-to-one with a child and then feeds back, perhaps in the form of a report, to the child's parents, teachers and others in the school, it is important to highlight that the underlying philosophy and concepts of dynamic assessment can, and should, be used in other ways. For example, the ideas of mediated learning might be imparted to teaching staff through training, the checklists of cognitive and affective factors on learning might form the basis of a consultation between an educational psychologist and the school, or the concepts of the cognitive and affective factors in learning might be taught to the whole class in order to develop these skills in *all* children. Throughout this book, we will outline the different ways that the resources can be used, over and above the more traditional notion of dynamic assessment.

Despite the concept of dynamic assessment being around for more than 50 years (Reuven

Feuerstein first published his ideas on an assisted assessment framework in 1968), it is still an approach that has not quite penetrated the everyday practice of educational psychologists in the UK (Callicott, Towers & Limniotis, 2020; Green & Birch, 2019; Hill, 2015), although it is argued that significant progress has been made in recent years (Stringer, 2018).

The staged process of dynamic assessment

Let's for a moment reflect on the more traditional approach to dynamic assessment, and by this we mean that, as a practitioner, you might be asked to do some assessment work with a particular child because of concerns regarding their learning (however, as stated above and as we will outline below, there will be other ways in which you may wish to use the ideas and concepts underlying dynamic assessment work). In this more traditional approach, we find it helpful to think of the process of dynamic assessment as consisting of four stages, as previously outlined in *Improving Learning Through Dynamic Assessment* (Lauchlan & Carrigan, 2013). The four steps of the staged process are: 1) Assessment, 2) Feedback, 3) Intervention, and 4) Review. In other words, first you carry out the dynamic assessment, then you feed back your results and conclusions to those working with the child (and the child themselves), and make an action plan for moving forward. Next there is a period of intervention where the action plan is executed in the classroom and perhaps with support at home, and finally, built into the process there is a review after several months to see if the intervention plan is working. Contained within this book are ideas and resources to help with these stages, and in particular stages 1 and 2.

CHAPTER 2

MEDIATED LEARNING

Background and theory

Mediated learning is based on the principle that learning usually occurs within a social and cultural context, where the child is able to interact with adults and their peers. Part of the concept of mediated learning is that the adult, or 'more able peer', has a key role in enabling effective learning. The development of mediated learning is heavily based on Vygotsky's (1978, 1986) framework of socio-cultural theory, and his concept of the Zone of Proximal Development (described in Chapter 1).

The theory of mediated learning was developed in direct contrast to previously considered theories of learning, mostly developed by Jean Piaget, where a child learns by working alone, almost like a lone scientist, actively constructing hypotheses and testing them out. It was felt that Piaget's theories underplayed the importance of the social and cultural context in which children learn, and in particular Piaget was criticized for how much he overlooked the key role of the adult or 'mediator' in helping children to learn.

As stated above, the alternative viewpoint to Piaget, in particular the concept of mediated learning, originated from the work of the Russian developmental psychologist Lev Vygotsky in the 1930s and the later work of psychologists such as Jerome Bruner and Margaret Donaldson in the 1970s and 1980s. Vygotsky's work was suppressed for many years because his views were considered to be so controversial, which is why the impact of his work was not seen until the 1970s and 1980s (unfortunately Vygotsky died in 1934 when he was only 38 years old).

Vygotsky's theories challenged the work of developmental psychologists such as Piaget and others and challenged a perspective which was prevalent for many years (and some might argue still promoted), that intelligence is something you are born with, it cannot be modified, and can be accurately assessed through the use of cognitive assessments (IQ tests). Vygotsky instead discussed how intelligence can only be accurately understood if you take into consideration the culture in which the child resides. Moreover, that intelligence can best be understood by assessing not only the products of the child's learning at the point of assessment, but also those developing cognitive processes (and as illustrated by his depiction of the Zones of Actual, Proximal and Potential Development).

With the influence of Vygotsky's work, Bruner and Donaldson (among others) began to investigate how children learn in a social context. They conducted several research studies and published several scientific papers and books (Bruner, 1977, 1995; Bruner & Haste, 1987; Donaldson, 1978; Wood, Bruner & Ross, 1976) that led to a 'quiet revolution', which involved promoting an alternative view as to how children learn – in other words, focusing on the *social* nature of learning.

As argued above, the role of an adult (or able peer) in this learning process was somewhat overlooked by Piaget. Instead, the work of Jerome Bruner and Margaret Donaldson highlighted that children learn through their interactions with those around them.

The social nature of learning is fundamentally important and has led to significant developments in how classrooms are set up, with a focus on children interacting and learning from each other.

In the 1940s and 1950s, an Israeli psychologist named Reuven Feuerstein developed a different way to assess and develop children's learning potential. He called this dynamic assessment. Similar to what was written above about Vygotsky, Feuerstein based his *theory of structural cognitive modifiability* (Feuerstein, Rand & Hoffman, 1979) on the idea that intelligence should not be thought of as a fixed, static entity, but instead that it can change and be modified, given the right circumstances and the right 'teaching' (or mediated learning).

Feuerstein felt that it was important to assess a child's 'ability to learn', rather than what they have learned up to the point of assessment (which is what standardized cognitive ability tests do, such as traditional IQ tests, which focus on individual, unassisted performance). He developed an alternative form of cognitive testing, which led to the birth of dynamic assessment.

Dynamic assessment is now used by educational psychologists and other professional groups all over the world as a means of assessing children's strengths and abilities, with a focus on the next steps of a child's learning. In other words, professionals using the practitioner approach to dynamic assessment are trying to answer the question: what can we do next to help this child?

The main focus of Feuerstein's work was on the theory of mediated learning, which had striking similarities to the work of Vygotsky and his notion of 'mediation'. Feuerstein and colleagues called their approach the 'mediated learning experience' (Feuerstein *et al.*, 1979; Feuerstein, Rand & Rynders, 1988).

Feuerstein's mediated learning experience

According to Reuven Feuerstein and his colleagues (1979, 1988) there are 11[1] components of mediated learning experiences:

1. Mediation of intentionality and reciprocity (or what we call...**engaging**). Ensuring that the child is aware that you are both working together and that the adult is working at the *child's level* of understanding. The child must be keen and interested in the task.
2. Mediation of meaning (or what we call...**making sense**). The child knows *why* they are doing the task.
3. Mediation of transcendence (or what we call...**bridging**). This can be described as the adult providing a *bridge* from the current experience to something that the child is able to relate to – either something from the past, or something in the future.

---

[1] It is acknowledged here that these 11 components or parameters of the Mediated Learning Experience have been slightly changed and updated over the years, in terms of the wording (e.g. 'Mediation of change' has become 'Mediation of the awareness of the human being as a changing entity' and there has been the addition of 'Mediation of the feeling of belonging' in the 2002 book *The Dynamic Assessment of Cognitive Modifiability* (Feuerstein *et al.*, 2002), making 12 components in total.

4. Mediation of feelings of competence (or what we call...**encouraging**). The importance of giving the child frequent, genuine and positive praise or encouragement. This should provide the child with *meaningful explicit feedback* so that the child knows what they are doing right and well.

5. Mediation of regulation and control of behaviour (or what we call...**self-regulation**). The adult inhibits impulsive behaviour and encourages the child to *regulate their own reflective behaviour* with comments such as 'Slow down', 'Take your time' and 'You know you do better when you stop and think about it'.

6. Mediation of sharing behaviour (or what we call...**sharing**). The adult emphasizes that they and the child are doing the task as *learning partners*: 'We're doing this together.'

7. Mediation of individuation and psychological differentiation (or what we call...**independence**). This is the flip side to mediation of sharing behaviour. If an adult takes sharing behaviour too far then it can result in the adult dominating the mediated learning and thus the child not being able to develop feelings of autonomy and independence. So, the mediator needs to know when to step back from the shared experience and allow the child to become a more independent learner.

8. Mediation of goal seeking, goal setting and goal achieving (or what we call...**planning, monitoring, explaining, verbalizing**). These involve different metacognitive aspects to the mediation. Children are encouraged to plan their problem-solving behaviour, check their answers, provide explanations as to how they solve the problems, and verbalize their way through the tasks.

9. Mediation of challenge (or what we call...**challenging, scaffolding**). It is an important aspect of learning that the child is working on tasks that will have some level of challenge but at the same time will not overwhelm them. Because the mediator is there to provide appropriate support, it is possible to reach into the Zone of Proximal Development and do more difficult tasks. The mediator can remove the 'scaffolding' as the child develops more autonomy.

10. Mediation of change (or what we call...**change**). This is about promoting the new skills the child has learned, and reflecting back to the child the progress that they have made.

11. Mediation of an optimistic alternative (or what we call...**positive outlook**). Sometimes the way we mediate does not work for the child. It's okay to change your methodology and try another way. 'I can see that this approach is not helping you to understand. Let's try another different way which may be more helpful.'

MEDIATED LEARNING IN FOCUS: THE BOY AND THE MUSHROOM

Imagine a young boy out on a country walk with his mother. During the walk the mum turns around and sees that her son has picked a wild mushroom and is about to place it in his mouth to eat it.

'STOP!' the mum shouts. 'Don't eat that!'

The little boy gets a fright and throws the mushroom away.

The mum's intervention is successful in averting any imminent danger that the boy is about to eat a poisonous mushroom. But, has the little boy learned anything? Will he spot something else

further on in the country walk and just as easily place it in his mouth to eat it without making sure that it's edible?

The mum has to intervene and engage in some mediated learning so that learning can take place. The dialogue might go something like this:

Mum: 'Listen, the reason I told you not to eat the mushroom is that it could have been poisonous. It could have made you really, really sick. You might even have ended up in hospital.'

Boy: 'What do you mean, Mum? We eat mushrooms all the time.'

Mum: 'Yes, that's true, we do, but we don't just pick them from the fields, do we? We buy them at the grocers, or the supermarket.'

Boy: 'Yes, we do. [thinks for a few seconds] But, wait a minute, old Mr McGregor, the neighbour from next door, goes out to the fields to pick mushrooms. He says he eats them. In fact, he says they're delicious.'

Mum: 'Well, yes, perhaps he does darling, but you see the difference is that Mr McGregor knows which mushrooms are okay to eat, and which ones are not okay to eat and could make you sick. You see, there are different kinds of mushrooms, and it's important to know the differences before you try to eat them.'

Boy: 'Ah, okay, I didn't know that. So, how can you tell the difference? Is there any way of knowing?'

Mum: 'Well, you can follow this rule. Your grandfather told me this when I was your age, and it seems to work. If you see a mushroom and it's among a clump of mushrooms where none of them have been touched, you know, munched or half-eaten by the wildlife around, then don't you eat it either. Instead, if you see a mushroom and it's among other mushrooms that have been eaten by the wildlife, then it'll likely be okay for you too.'

Boy: 'Okay, I think I'm starting to get it now. So basically, there are some kinds that are okay to eat and other kinds that are not.'

Mum: 'Exactly. You've got it. But it's not only for mushrooms. The same goes for anything that we see out here in the countryside. Apples, berries, lettuces, and so on. There will be kinds that are okay, and other kinds that are not okay, so you'll have to make sure that you've picked the kind that is okay to eat.'

Boy: 'So, you mean, is it like that day we went out to pick brambles to make jelly? I remember we didn't stop at the first ones that we saw that day. We kept going until we found the right ones.'

Mum: 'That's exactly right, darling. Well done. You remembered. That's the kind of thing I mean. I'm really impressed you made that connection. So, just remember it counts for all things that we see out in the wild. That's something new you've learned today. Some kinds we can eat, but other kinds of the same fruit or vegetable we can't eat.'

The true test of the effectiveness of the mediated learning would be further on in the country walk when the boy spots some berries. If the mum did not engage in mediated learning as outlined above, and merely told him to throw the mushroom away, what would the boy do? The most likely consequence would be that he would just as easily pop the berries in his mouth without checking things out with his mum first. Instead, if the mum engaged in the mediated learning as described above, it is more likely that the boy would come running to his mum and say, 'Look, Mum, I've spotted some berries. Are these the kind that are okay or not okay to eat?'

This anecdote illustrates that mediated learning can be done by anyone: parents, teachers, teaching assistants, educational psychologists, speech therapists, and many others. Mediated learning is about ensuring that learning takes place. But let's analyse this anecdote in greater detail, in relation to some of the Mediated Learning Principles.

- Mediation of intentionality and reciprocity (Engaging) – there is clear evidence in the dialogue of a reciprocal nature to the experience by both mother and child. The boy is asking questions and is clearly engaged. The mum is keeping focused on imparting the lesson about edible and inedible foods in the wild.
- Mediation of meaning (Making sense) – the mum is promoting meaning to the interaction, namely that the boy has to learn about edible and inedible foods.
- Mediation of transcendence (Bridging) – the mum makes links to possible future experiences (apples, berries and lettuces), making the learning relevant and concrete, rather than abstract. The boy makes a connection with a previous experience picking brambles.
- Mediation of feelings of competence (Encouraging) – the mum praises the child for his level of understanding ('Exactly. You've got it') and for remembering about the day they picked brambles for jelly, reinforcing the fact that he made the link by himself ('I'm really impressed you made that connection').
- Mediation of regulation and control of behaviour (Self-regulation) – the mum doesn't jump in to interrupt the boy's thinking when he takes a few seconds to remember about the neighbour Mr McGregor's mushroom-picking habits.
- Mediation of sharing behaviour (Sharing) – the mum shares the experience of what the boy's grandfather told her when she was little. She makes sure this is told in his terms ('your grandfather', rather than 'my father'). Her language is predominantly using 'we' ('we buy them at the grocers' and 'the same goes for anything that we see out here in the countryside').
- Mediation of individuation and psychological differentiation (Independence) – an example implied in the above anecdote would be allowing the child to walk a little on his own and spot potential foodstuff independently, in the expectation that he will come to his mum to check if they're edible.
- Mediation of goal seeking, goal setting and goal achieving (Planning) – while not specified in the above anecdote, some planning could be encouraged through the following – 'How much walking do you think we'll do today?' – and during the walk: 'How far do you think we've walked up to now?', 'How much further do you think we still have to go?'
- Mediation of change (Change) – the mum reinforces that the boy has learned something new during the dialogue, reiterating the meaning of the mediated learning. ('That's something new you've learned today. Some kinds we can eat, but other kinds of the same fruit or vegetable we can't eat.')

We're sure that many of you reading this anecdote will think, 'I do this all the time. This is just good teaching.' However, if we reflect on our teaching, or mediation, there

> may well be some Mediated Learning Principles that we use a lot, but others that we need to develop. It's important to always look to refine our mediated learning style and think about what we can do better. The worksheet in Chapter 7 (Resource 2.3) entitled Guide to Building Mediated Learning Competencies, and described further below, is designed to help you to do this.

Putting these ideas into practice

Theory is one thing, putting it into practice is another. Many of you will find that you are already putting Mediated Learning Principles into practice when working with children.

It might be useful to think about the following ways in which mediated learning can take place. We call these the 17 Mediated Learning Principles that have been adapted from Feuerstein's theory of mediated learning experience, but we have added some based on our 40 years of experience of using the dynamic assessment approach. In Table 2.1 we can see 1) the list of Mediated Learning Principles, 2) a short description of each framed as a question, 3) the definition using child-friendly language and 4) the image we use to represent each one.

Table 2.1: Mediated Learning Principles

Mediated Learning Principle	Short description	Child-friendly language	Representational image
Implicit help	Is the mediator only having to give small hints, clues and prompts in order to improve performance?	I can offer hints, clues and prompts	
Explicit help	Is the mediator having to give detailed feedback/assistance including explicit discussion of problem-solving strategies in order to improve performance?	I can give more detailed explanations if they are needed	

Engaging	Is the mediator trying to engage the child in a reciprocal interaction to ensure the answer is correct?	I can get others to become involved in a task	
Making sense	Is the mediator promoting meaningfulness in the task?	I can speak clearly and make sure things make sense for others	
Bridging	Is the mediator making links to previous or future experiences, for example what happens in the classroom?	I can help others see the links between the past, present and future	
Encouraging	Is the mediator giving frequent, enthusiastic praise and encouragement?	I am an encourager	

cont.

Mediated Learning Principle	Short description	Child-friendly language	Representational image
Self-regulation	Is the mediator trying to ensure that the child slows down, reflects and takes their time?	I can self-regulate and help others to self-regulate too	
Sharing	Is the mediator interacting in a way that communicates that they are on the child's side, that they are working together as a team?	I can work as part of a team	
Independence	Is the mediator taking a step back allowing the child to take over?	I encourage and support others to do things on their own	
Planning	Is the mediator encouraging planning (no one plans to fail, they only fail to plan)?	I can role model good planning	

Monitoring	Is the mediator ensuring that the child is checking their answers?	I can help others keep an eye on their progress	
Explaining	Is the mediator asking for explanations, guiding the child to justify their answers?	I can help others to give good explanations for their answers	
Verbalizing	Is the mediator encouraging the child to talk aloud when doing the tasks in order to highlight their thinking?	I can model how to verbalize your way through tasks	
Scaffolding	Is the mediator gradually building up skills, giving less and less help until the child takes over responsibility for learning?	I can scaffold learning	

cont.

Mediated Learning Principle	Short description	Child-friendly language	Representational image
Challenging	Is the mediator ensuring that tasks are challenging, without overwhelming the child?	I can provide the right level of challenge	
Change	Is the mediator highlighting new skills that have been learned?	I can help others see the changes they have made in their work	
Positive outlook	Is the mediator always maintaining a positive outlook despite difficulties?	I can help others see the positives	

These 17 Mediated Learning Principles have been put together in a checklist for you to use when doing dynamic assessment – see Resource 2.1: Checklist of Mediated Learning Principles in Chapter 7.

How can I help the child to learn?

As you will have seen, mediated learning is not rocket science. It's something that happens every day in the classroom and at home with parents and carers, perhaps without the mediator realizing it.

Although language forms an important part in the mediated learning process, this doesn't mean that you can't use other concrete and visual methods to supplement teaching and learning.

It's important to note that mediated learning is not meant to be a method to encourage dependence from an adult. Rather the opposite. You are helping the child to develop skills that enable them to become more independent learners.

Reuven Feuerstein (Feuerstein *et al.*, 2002) proposed that any child, irrespective of their needs, can develop skills through mediated learning. It is a very positive outlook on how children can learn new things every day and that their intelligence is *not* fixed and immutable. Instead, there are always possibilities for change and new beginnings.

When working with children with additional learning needs, adapt your approach to suit their needs and ability. It is okay to have high expectations, but also, we need to be realistic about what the child can achieve.

However small a step may look to you, it may be a HUGE achievement for the child.

Each Mediated Learning Principle can be broken down further, for example...

Bridging (Transcendence)

A key goal in mediated learning is to develop transfer or bridging which occurs when an interaction goes beyond the immediate context or task and the learner is able to transfer the knowledge gained through mediation to other areas in their life. Every single activity has the potential for transference.

Mediation of transference – or bridging – involves:

- finding frameworks and generalizable rules that apply to similar situations
- bridging or linking events from the past to the present and the future
- being able to reflect and develop an understanding of the situation or context presented
- adopting a lateral thinking approach to learning (thinking outside the box).

Resources to help you with mediated learning

In Chapter 7, you will find the following resources, each of which has a description of how to use them with the intended goal of developing skills and competencies in mediated learning:

- Resource 2.1: Checklist of Mediated Learning Principles
- Resource 2.2: Checklist of Mediated Learning Principles – Rating Scale
- Resource 2.3: Guide to Building Mediated Learning Competencies

Summary

In this chapter, we have discussed theories of developmental psychology and, in particular, the work of Lev Vygotsky and Reuven Feuerstein, and how their theories have had an impact on our understanding of how children learn. Specifically, we have considered the theory of mediation, or mediated learning, and what this looks like in practice. It is this approach to working with children that can be a powerful tool in the classroom and in the assessment context. However, there are other aspects to learning that we must consider as part of our Dynamic Triad of Effective Learning: the cognitive and affective/emotional skills of the child or young person (Chapter 3) and the tools or materials that we use when working with them (Chapter 4). A fundamentally important element is how to effect positive change too, and this is covered in Chapter 5.

CHAPTER 3

COGNITIVE AND AFFECTIVE LEARNING PRINCIPLES

Cognitive aspects to learning

When a child is engaged in a task, we can observe several aspects of their learning behaviour and how they approach that task. And moreover, when as adults we are working with the child, then these aspects of their problem-solving behaviour can change and be 'modified' as a result of the mediated learning provided. Vygotsky (1978) called these aspects the 'cognitive processes' or 'cognitive functions' of the child, and he described how important it is to consider not only those cognitive aspects of behaviour that are fully developed, but also those that are in the process of developing. His story of the gardener and the orchard, adapted here for the purposes of this textbook, beautifully highlights the difference between cognitive products and processes.

> **THE GARDENER AND THE ORCHARD (ADAPTED FROM VYGOTSKY, 1978)**
>
> Imagine there's a gardener working in an orchard. He knows that his boss is coming to visit soon to check his work and assess how the orchard is coming along. The gardener works overtime, doing his best to make a good impression on his boss, watering the trees, talking to them, pruning them, doing everything possible to make the orchard look good.
>
> The day arrives when the boss comes for his visit. He says to the gardener, 'Right, talk me through the orchard. What's the situation?' What does the gardener do? He starts off with the trees that have the fully grown, fully ripened fruit hanging from the branches: 'Look in that corner over there. Can you see the oranges? Look at the size of them. They're delicious, so juicy. They're ready to be picked…and look in the other corner. The apple tree. Look at the colour of those apples. They're wonderful. Go and try one.'
>
> Now, the gardener has been working overtime. He wants to do his hard work some justice. He doesn't only want to concentrate on a couple of trees, only those that are fully grown with the fruit hanging from the branches. So, he begins to talk about the other trees that he's been working on too. 'See over there, next to the apple trees, I know you can't quite see yet, but that's an apricot tree. I've been tending to that one very carefully and it's coming along nicely. I'm telling you, in a few weeks you're going

> to have some delicious apricots in that tree... Same with that other one in the other corner. It's a pear tree. It needs a bit more time, but you'll see some tasty pears dangling from the branches in a week or two. I can tell it's going to be a cracker.'
>
> Vygotsky said we need to discuss how children learn and their cognitive development in the same way as the gardener. If we only focus on what children are able to do independently, then we are only considering the fully developed cognitive skills (or products), in other words those competencies that are fully grown and fully matured. Instead, we need to consider the cognitive skills that are in the process of developing, those that are not fully matured, that are under the surface. These skills are revealed in collaborative activity, when an adult or more able peer works with a child and provides mediated learning. Once we get access to these developing cognitive skills then it provides us with richer, more powerful information that can help us to advise best on the next steps of the child's learning. The theory is that we should focus on these developing skills and competencies in order to make a difference in the classroom.

Leontiev, a contemporary of Vygotsky's, said that too often in education we focus on where the child is *now* (vis-à-vis the assessment of individual performance using standardized cognitive ability tests), but instead we should be focusing on discovering how the child can become what they not yet are, in other words reaching into the Zone of Proximal Development through the provision of mediated learning by an adult or more able peer (Leontiev, 1977). In fact, Vygotsky (1978, p.89) wrote that 'the only "good learning" is that which is in advance of development', and it is this theoretical stance that encompasses our work in dynamic assessment. Before we go any further, we feel it is important to address the similarities between the notion of cognitive functions, or processes, and the concept of executive functions, as they are closely related.

The concept of executive functioning was first introduced in the 1970s (Pribram, 1973) to describe core aspects of behaviour that are controlled by the prefrontal cortex functions of the brain. Initially the description of executive functions revolved around key aspects of behaviour such as planning, decision-making, purposeful action and the generation of effective performance, as opposed to the passive assimilation of information (Reynolds & Horton, 2006). Research into executive functions has multiplied in recent years and it is now a well-established concept in developmental and cognitive psychology.

Naglieri and Goldstein (2013) developed the notion of executive functions further, and their Comprehensive Executive Functioning Inventory (CEFI) allows for the examination of how children and young people engage in problem-solving behaviour and knowledge acquisition. The CEFI focuses on nine areas: planning, self-monitoring, organization, memory, attention, flexibility, initiation, inhibitory control and emotion regulation. The links between research into executive functions and the work of Vygotsky and Feuerstein, in relation to cognitive functions, are clear. One might argue that they are exploring the same aspects of problem-solving behaviour, only using different terminology. For example, Diamond (2013) breaks down some of the executive functions further, some of which we would argue are identical concepts to some of our Cognitive and Affective Learning Principles. Table 3.1 shows some examples.

Table 3.1: Executive Functions versus Cognitive and Affective Learning Principles

Diamond's (2013) Executive Functions	Lauchlan and Carrigan's (2013) Cognitive and Affective Learning Principles
Mentally playing with ideas	Exploratory behaviour
Taking the time to think before acting	Reflectiveness
Meeting novel, unanticipated challenges	Frustration tolerance
Resisting temptations	Concentration
Staying focused	Attention

Working memory and cognitive flexibility are also outlined by Diamond (2013), both of which are considered in our model of Cognitive and Affective Learning Principles, which will be described in full detail below.

Feuerstein *et al.* (1979, 2002) labelled the cognitive processes and products as 'deficient cognitive functions'. In fact, Feuerstein and colleagues divided problem-solving behaviour into three distinct phases: the Input Phase, where information is gathered, the Elaboration Phase, where the information is elaborated on, and then the Output Phase, where the solution to the problem or task is communicated. He delineated 27 of these deficient cognitive functions in total: eight at the Input Phase, eleven at the Elaboration Phase and eight at the Output Phase. Here are some examples: 'Unplanned, impulsive and unsystematic exploratory behaviour'; 'Lack of, or deficient, need for precision and accuracy in data gathering'; 'Inability to select relevant vs. irrelevant cues in defining a problem'; 'Deficiencies in visual transport' (Feuerstein *et al.*, 2002, pp.138–140).

Feuerstein *et al.*'s (2002) description of these aspects of cognitive behaviour has had a huge impact on our own work in dynamic assessment; however, one thing that is noticeable is that the deficient cognitive functions were worded negatively. In *Improving Learning Through Dynamic Assessment* (Lauchlan & Carrigan, 2013), we described how we adapted these deficient cognitive functions, and one of the main purposes was to turn the language on its head and phrase the cognitive aspects of learning in a positive way. The rationale underlying this decision was that wording the cognitive aspects of learning positively would be more compatible with our everyday educational psychology practice (based on positive psychology) and would reflect the philosophy in the local authority's educational psychology services where we worked. Our educational psychology practice was embedded in positive psychology (Seligman & Csikszentmihalyi, 2000; Seligman *et al.*, 2005) and in particular the solution-focused brief therapy approach (Ratner, George & Iveson, 2012), which underpinned the vast majority of our work in nursery, primary and secondary schools in the local authority. Positive psychology and solution-focused methods embrace an approach that focuses on strengths rather than deficits, on moving forwards rather than problems, on engaging and empowering children, and a focus on what is working well, rather than what is not working (Bozic, 2013; Noble & McGrath, 2008). These are all characteristics of the dynamic assessment approach too. Thus, we felt it was important that our assessment framework also reflected a similar positively minded approach to our work with children and young people.

In fact, it became a natural process for us to consider how dialogue plays such an important role in dynamic assessment, through the practice of mediated learning. As Clark (2008)

argued, 'talk is a form of mind-transforming cognitive scaffolding' (p.44). Clark argued further that dialogue can play a key role in learning, yet it is an approach that remains 'surprisingly ill understood' (p.44). The links between mediated learning and working in a therapeutic context are perhaps more obvious than we might first consider.

Educational psychologists use talk or dialogue in many different approaches to therapeutic work, usually when working with children and young people's social, emotional and mental health needs. But can talk and dialogue also be effective when working with children who have learning problems? One of the purposes of mediated learning is to engage in a much deeper analysis of the child's learning, and this might also include talking with the child or young person about their learning – which aspects they feel are strengths (one might say, those that are in the Zone of Actual Development), which aspects they find more difficult (those that are in the Zone of Potential Development), and which ones are in the process of emerging (in the Zone of Proximal Development). The resources in this book are designed to help you to explore these aspects of learning in different ways and in a variety of contexts. Of course, like any therapeutic talk-based approach, we accept that how this can help a child with their learning will depend on several factors, most importantly the age and stage of the child, and whether they are able to engage productively with such methods. Thus, the use of elaborate dialogue as an approach to dynamic assessment may only be appropriate for certain children.

Emotional aspects to learning

Only focusing on cognitive aspects of learning can undermine the significance of emotional, or affective, factors. In fact, Tzuriel, Samuels and Feuerstein (1988) recognized this and highlighted that the original model of deficient cognitive functions overlooked these factors. Their argument was that we should also be exploring any non-intellective – or affective – factors in how the child is learning a task. They outlined seven non-intellective factors that should be a focus of a dynamic assessment: accessibility to mediation, need for mastery (motivation), frustration tolerance, locus of control, fear of failure and defensiveness, confidence in correct responses, and vitality and alertness (see Tzuriel *et al.*, 1988, for more details).

In developing our own list of Cognitive and Affective Learning Principles, as stated above, we wanted to make sure that all of the learning principles were worded positively. And while we acknowledged the huge influence of Feuerstein *et al.* (1979, 2002) and Tzuriel *et al.* (1988) in our work, we felt it was necessary to remove some factors from their original lists, insert some of our own ideas, adapt the language, and also make sure that each of the learning principles were defined clearly and simply. Indeed, this led to the development of our list using child-friendly language and graphic representations of each, so that *all* stakeholders can become involved in the assessment and intervention process.

In Table 3.2 we can see 1) the list of Cognitive Learning Principles, 2) a short description of each framed as a question, 3) the definition using child-friendly language and 4) the image we use to represent each one.

Table 3.2: Cognitive Learning Principles

Cognitive Learning Principle	Short description	Child-friendly language	Representational image
Communication	Is the child communicating their answers in a clear and coherent manner?	I communicate my answers in a clear way	
Comparative behaviour	Is the child comparing objects, noticing what is similar/different?	I can spot when things are the same and different	
Efficiency	Is the child working at a reasonable pace rather than taking excessive time to ensure the answer is correct?	I work without rushing or taking too long	
Exploratory behaviour	Is the child searching for solutions rather than settling on the first one that comes to mind?	I can search for answers to problems	

cont.

Cognitive Learning Principle	Short description	Child-friendly language	Representational image

Cognitive Learning Principle	Short description	Child-friendly language	Representational image
Justification of response	Is the child able to justify their responses; that is, explain how they solved the problem?	I can explain how I get my answers	
Memory	Is the child able to remember information/ strategies sufficiently, in order to complete tasks?	I can remember information that will help me with my work	
Nature of response	Is the child answering with meaning rather than guessing randomly?	I can choose my answers carefully	
Planning	Is the child using a plan or strategy to solve the problem?	I am able to plan my steps to solve a problem	

Problem definition	Is the child showing that they understand the nature of the task?	I can understand what I am being asked to do	
Recognition	Is the child able to recognize when answers are incorrect?	I notice when my answers are not correct	
Reflectiveness	Is the child pausing to reflect on their answers?	I take time to think about my answers	
Spatial awareness	Is the child aware of positioning, left and right and coordination?	I can understand positions and know my left and right	

cont.

Cognitive Learning Principle	Short description	Child-friendly language	Representational image
Transfer of learning	Is the child able to transfer the learning from one problem to the next?	I can use what I have learned to help me with other tasks	
Vocabulary	Is the child labelling the information using the appropriate vocabulary?	I use the correct words when naming things	

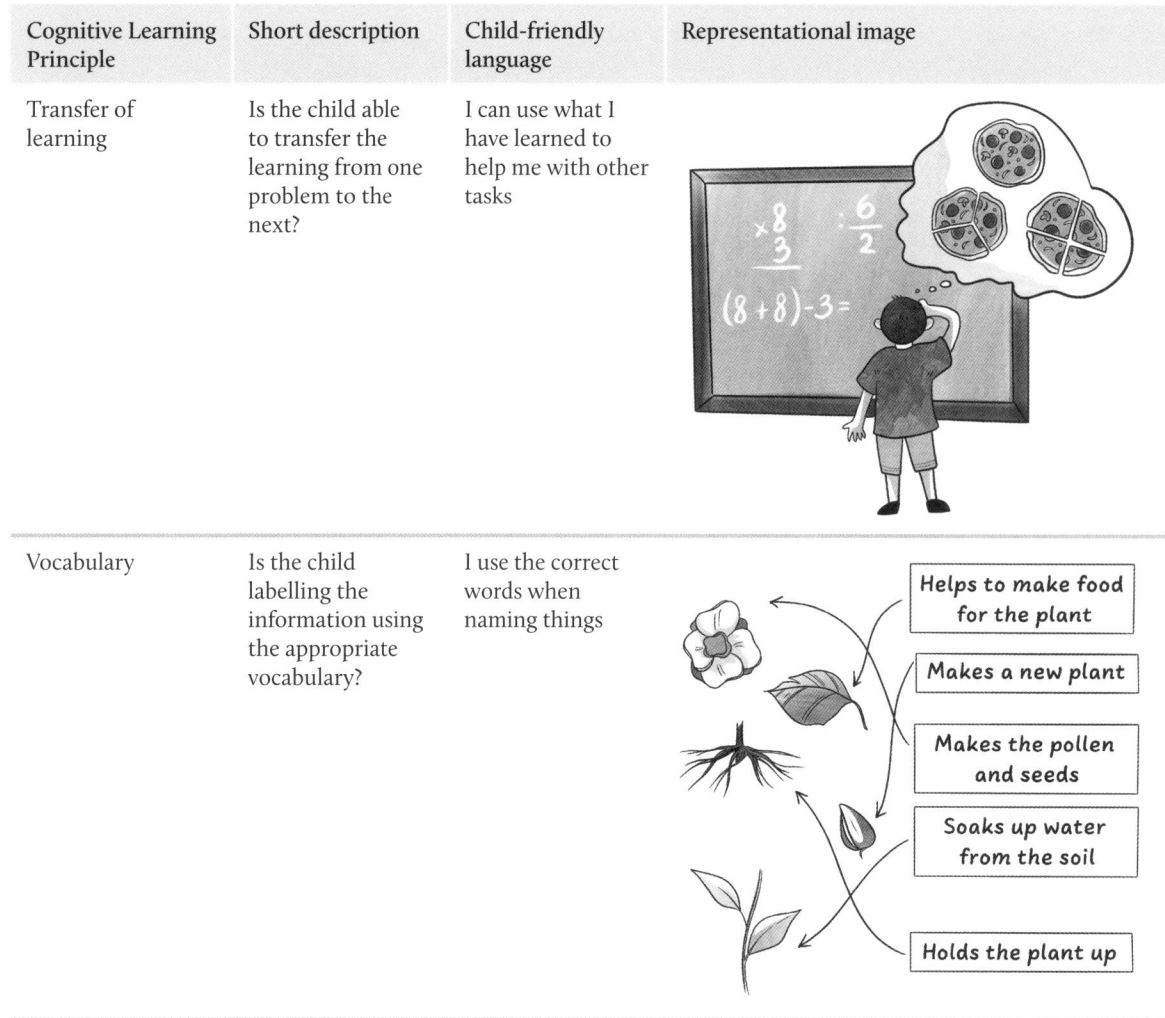

In Table 3.3 we can see 1) the list of Affective Learning Principles, 2) a short description of each framed as a question, 3) the definition using child-friendly language and 4) the image we use to represent each one.

Table 3.3: Affective Learning Principles

Affective Learning Principle	Short description	Child-friendly language	Representational image
Accessible to assistance	Is the child seeking help, prompting assistance and willing to become involved in a collaborative exchange?	I can ask for help when I need it	

COGNITIVE AND AFFECTIVE LEARNING PRINCIPLES | 37

Attention	Is the child able to sustain attention for a significant period of time?	I can keep my mind on my work and not be distracted	
Concentration	Is the child able to focus and remain concentrated on the task?	I can stay interested in tasks	
Confidence in correct responses	Is the child answering with conviction, sticking to their answers when challenged?	I can stick to my answers when challenged	
Flexibility	Is the child flexible in their use of strategies and in their general way of working, e.g. are they able to change how they approach a problem?	I can change the way in which I try to solve a problem	
Frustration tolerance	Is the child attempting problems/tasks regardless of perceived difficulty, e.g. are they keen to try?	I give my work a try even when it looks difficult	

cont.

Affective Learning Principle	Short description	Child-friendly language	Representational image
Motivation	Is the child keen to perform well?	I want to do well in school tasks	
Presentation	Is the child relaxed/comfortable?	I feel relaxed and comfortable when I'm learning	
Task perseverance	Is the child continuing to work on the task despite encountering difficulties?	I keep going with my work even if it is difficult	
Vitality and awareness	Is the child eager, full of energy and alert?	I am awake and ready to learn	

Affective Learning Principle	Short description	Child-friendly language	Representational image

In Chapter 7 (Resources), you will find the Cognitive and Affective Learning Principles presented in the form of different checklists and rating scales, with the purpose of using them in different ways:

- Resource 3.1: Checklist of Cognitive Learning Principles
- Resource 3.2: Checklist of Affective Learning Principles
- Resource 3.3: Rating Scale of Cognitive Learning Principles (Adult Version)
- Resource 3.4: Rating Scale of Affective Learning Principles (Adult Version)
- Resource 3.5: Rating Scale of Cognitive Learning Principles (Child-friendly Version)
- Resource 3.6: Rating Scale of Affective Learning Principles (Child-friendly Version)

Summary

In this chapter, we have considered the aspects of problem-solving behaviour, sometimes referred to as cognitive functions, or executive functions, that children engage in when learning. We have also discussed the emotional factors that appear in learning, and that can help or interfere with the child's cognitive capacities. We frame these concepts under the umbrella of 24 Cognitive and Affective Learning Principles. These learning principles can provide a focus for dynamic assessment and intervention work. In the following chapters, we will consider how this can be done and how this can lead to important, positive changes to the child's learning in the classroom.

CHAPTER 4

DYNAMIC ASSESSMENT MATERIALS

Reflecting back on the Dynamic Triad of Effective Learning (Figure 1.1), we have discussed mediated learning (Chapter 2), and the Cognitive and Affective Learning Principles of the learner (Chapter 3). This chapter will focus on the task or content used when doing dynamic assessment with a child or young person.

Our view is that you can use any content that will allow you to explore as effectively as possible the child's learning and the ways in which they respond to mediated learning. This task might even be something that the child is working on in the classroom, perhaps a literacy task, or a mathematics problem. Some educational psychologists may even do dynamic assessment 'in situ'; in other words, while doing some classroom observation, they may intervene and engage in mediated learning with whichever task the child is working on at that time.

Some educational psychologists use the subtests from any given standardized cognitive ability test in a dynamic way. This means that rather than administering the subtests as indicated by the test manual (with a standard script and no interaction with the child that might improve performance, including the provision of feedback), the assessor will instead intervene, provide mediated learning, and then see the level that the child can reach with help. While this might be a useful way to carry out dynamic assessment as perhaps the psychologist is familiar with the test materials and has an idea of the level that a child might reach, one does have to be careful with the use of this kind of content, as it may interfere with any eventual standardized administration of the same test in the future. Repeated exposure to the same content will affect performance, and if the standardized cognitive ability test is to be administered in the manner intended (that is, to compare performance with the norm for the age group), then the use of the cognitive ability subtests administered in a dynamic way will compromise such results.

There are specific dynamic assessment materials available, many of which (including the ones described below) are currently used by educational psychologists in the UK (see Green & Birch, 2019, and Stringer, 2018, for further discussion on this). Here are some materials that could be considered.

The Learning Propensity Assessment Device (LPAD), originally called the Learning Potential Assessment Device (Feuerstein *et al.*, 1979, 2002), was arguably the first dynamic assessment test to emerge. It consists of 14 subtests, including the Organization of Dots, the Complex Figure Drawing, the Word Memory test and the Representational Stencil Design test. Availability of these materials is limited to those who attend official training and workshops organized by the International Center for the Enhancement of Learning Potential, based in Jerusalem, Israel. The training covers the theoretical and conceptual background to dynamic assessment and how these instruments can be used in practice.

Professor David Tzuriel has designed several dynamic assessment test materials, including the Cognitive Modifiability Battery (CMB) (Tzuriel, 1995), the Children's Analogical Thinking Modifiability test (CATM) (Tzuriel & Klein, 1985), and the Children's Inferential Thinking Modifiability test (CITM) (Tzuriel, 1992). The CMB consists of four wooden boards and wooden blocks that come in four colours and four different heights. There are a number of subtests that can be used with the CMB, including analogical reasoning, sequential reasoning, and memory. The materials can be used with children and young people of all ages as the tasks vary in complexity. The CATM instead is targeted at younger children and consists of large and small wooden blocks that come in three colours (yellow, red and blue) and three shapes (squares, circles and triangles). Once the dimensions are established with the child the assessor can engage in analogical reasoning tasks, which are laid out on cards that come as part of the test materials. The CITM is a task that requires inferential thinking (if...then reasoning). Children have to work out which objects should go into different houses that are distinguished by different coloured roofs by making inferences using the information provided. Tzuriel has developed several other dynamic assessment tools, including the Children's Seriational Thinking Modifiability test (CSTM) (Tzuriel, 1993), the Children's Conceptual and Perceptual Analogical Modifiability test (CCPAM) (Tzuriel & Galinka, 2002), and the Seria-Think test (Tzuriel, 1999). As with the LPAD, availability of these materials is limited to those who attend Professor Tzuriel's training and workshops, where live demonstrations of these materials are shown along with the practical applications for educational psychologists. Professor Tzuriel continues to provide workshops on how to use these instruments all over the world and regularly in the UK.

What do you do if these specific dynamic assessment materials are not available? As stated above, dynamic assessment can be used with any task or content, even something that the child is already working on in the classroom. Alternatively, there are several problem-solving games designed to promote thinking skills in children that are available on the high street or online, some of which require higher-order conceptual thinking. It is not the purpose of this book to make specific suggestions about which games to purchase; however, anything that involves problem-solving/thinking skills can be used as a useful tool to carry out dynamic assessment. While the content of the task can be important, what is more important are 1) how the child responds to the mediated learning, 2) which Cognitive and Affective Learning Principles are displayed by the child (or produce change during the assessment), and 3) the identification of useful next steps for the child's learning.

In our work, we are often asked by teachers, and by educational psychologists during training, about the necessity to use a task in dynamic assessment that is curriculum-based, rather than a task that is removed from the usual content delivered in the classroom. For example, some teachers may argue that analogical reasoning, or games that involve problem-solving and thinking skills, do not accurately reflect what is expected of the child in class. There are two arguments to this. One is that in dynamic assessment we are aiming to explore the child's learning through optimal performance; in other words, we are reaching into the Zone of Proximal Development (ZPD). The use of content with which the child is already encountering difficulty will likely just confirm the child's difficulties in this area, and it will be more problematic for the mediator to reach into the ZPD. Instead, using a task or activity to which the child has never previously been exposed will mean that they will tackle the task with vigour and a level of interest that will allow the mediator to explore the ZPD and an optimal level of performance. The second argument lies in the generalizability of the Cognitive and Affective Learning Principles. If we have evidence that some of these learning principles are emerging in the child – such that they are displayed in an assisted assessment context – albeit in a task that is different from the usual curriculum-based content, then we can begin to consider how these learning principles can be encouraged in classroom work, where the learning principles will be just as fundamentally important to the child's success in that task.

We have included some tasks below, taken from the book *Improving Learning Through Dynamic Assessment* (Lauchlan & Carrigan, 2013), that you may find useful when doing dynamic assessment. These are directly related to some of the Cognitive Learning Principles, and the Affective Learning Principles can be observed and assessed too.

Memory Challenge

As the name suggests, this task is principally aimed at dynamically assessing memory, in a fun way. Full details of how to do this task – as well as the worksheets – are provided in Chapter 7, with some suggestions for providing mediated learning designed to improve the children's performance. The Cognitive and Affective Learning Principles assessed are also outlined in Chapter 7. Two different difficulty levels are provided: Resource 4.1 involves remembering 12 objects and Resource 4.2 involves remembering 20 objects. Suggestions for the kind of objects to use in this task are given in Resource 4.3.

Can You Colour?

This activity is also principally aimed at dynamically assessing working memory, but other learning principles can be explored as well. Full details of how to use this resource – as well as the worksheets – are provided in Chapter 7. The Cognitive and Affective Learning Principles that are assessed using this activity are also outlined. The task involves reading out aloud a sequence of colours to the child or young person and asking them to memorize them by colouring the worksheet provided. Different difficulty levels are available involving three (Resource 4.4), five (Resource 4.5) and nine (Resource 4.6) colours. Some ideas are given in Chapter 7 for how one might provide mediated learning when using this task. The task can also be adapted to drawing (Can you draw?), sculpting using play dough (Can you make?) and acting (Can you act?).

Picture Sequencing

This task is principally designed to dynamically assess the Cognitive Learning Principles of reflectiveness and planning; however, other learning principles can be explored too, which are detailed in Chapter 7. The child or young person is asked to think of an event (e.g. 'Getting ready for school', 'Travelling to school', 'What I did at the weekend', or 'What I did on holiday'), and is then asked to draw a representation of each part of the sequence on the worksheet (see Resources 4.7, 4.8, 4.9 and 4.10 in Chapter 7). Or they can write their responses or have an adult write for them. The task begins with a simpler version with just three steps (Resource 4.7), building up to a more complex version involving six steps (Resource 4.10). Alternatively, the child can write on the boxes provided, or their responses can be transcribed by the adult. Some suggestions for providing mediated learning when using the task are provided in Chapter 7, as well as how the task can be adapted and expanded.

Word Bingo

This task is principally aimed at dynamically assessing the Cognitive Learning Principles of communication and vocabulary, but other learning principles can be explored too, as outlined in Chapter 7. Word Bingo is similar to traditional bingo, but words are used rather than numbers, and instead of calling out the words, the mediator reads out a definition. The task can be helpful in assessing the language skills of a child in a fun way. Resources 4.11 (basic version) and 4.12 (advanced version) are provided in Chapter 7, as well as some ideas as to how mediated learning can be implemented. The task can be adapted and expanded by the adults working with the child.

Find Your Way

In this activity, the mediator can dynamically assess the Cognitive Learning Principles of spatial orientation and vocabulary, but other learning principles can also be explored using this task, as outlined in Chapter 7. The child is asked to provide directions from one landmark to another using a ready-made map (see Resource 4.13). Full details of the Cognitive and Affective Learning Principles that are usually observed on this task are given in Chapter 7, as well as more information as to how the activity can be used, including some suggestions for providing mediated learning.

I am Dynamic Cards

We have created cards that can also be used during dynamic assessment, available from our website www.dynamicassessmentuk.com. The cards depict the words and representational image of the 17 Mediated Learning Principles (as outlined in Table 2.1) and the 24 Cognitive and Affective Learning Principles (as outlined in Tables 3.2 and 3.3), and we have added 19 key concepts that can also be used as a stimulus for dialogue and discussion with a child or young person about their learning. The total number of cards is 60. The additional key concepts are outlined in Table 4.1. The 'I am Dynamic' cards can be used in different ways:

1. After doing some dynamic assessment work with the child, whether it's a problem-solving task, or the use of the specific dynamic assessment tools outlined above, or a classroom-based task, you can then begin to discuss the child's performance with reference to the cards. For example, after picking out the relevant card, 'I could see you were using a lot of planning during our work. Is this something you do in the classroom? Can you give me any examples? Or do you think this is something that you could do better?' or, 'I noticed how much more reflective you were at the end of our session, compared to when we started. You were taking your time more, thinking about what you were doing, and this made a huge difference to the quality of your work. Do you think this is something that we could work on together, perhaps trying to do this more in the classroom? Shall we consider putting this in our plan?' or, 'You became much more confident by the end of the session. Did you notice? Why do you think this was? Is this something that we could work on over the next few months?' and so on. The discussion using the cards can form the basis of the feedback and action plan, an essential part of dynamic assessment that is described in more detail in Chapter 5.
2. The cards can be used on their own, that is without the need for a specific problem-solving task. Instead, the cards become a stimulus for the dialogue about the child's learning, helping the child to reflect on their areas of strength, those areas where they sometimes need a little bit of help, and those that still require more intensive work. Of course, the success of this kind of approach will depend on the age and stage of the child or young person, but it can kickstart a useful way of enabling change in how the child learns, and what can be done differently.
3. Some of the cards can be selected given prior knowledge of the child's learning from the teacher and/or teaching assistant, and thus only a few are used to investigate how the child or young person works on some of these specific aspects of learning. The dialogue can then focus on next steps of learning, focusing only on these particular elements (or learning principles) previously identified. The results of the discussion then form the basis for the formulation of clearly definable goals that will represent next steps for the child's learning context (see Chapter 5 for further details on how to formulate DYNAMIC goals).

Table 4.1: List of key concepts that form part of the I am Dynamic Cards

1. Things that are important to me are…	11. One thing I can do today towards my goal is…
2. Things I can control…	12. I can flip a fail…
3. Things I can't control…	13. I can use technology…
4. Who notices what I do…	14. I believe in myself…
5. I have goals…	15. I believe in others…
6. I am in my zone when…	16. I respect others…
7. I am dynamic because…	17. I can collaborate…
8. I know how and where to ask for help…	18. I can look after our environment…
9. I am ready to learn when…	19. I am creative…
10. I bounce back when things don't go well first time…	

Summary

While we have described some materials that might be helpful for practitioners when carrying out dynamic assessment work and given some ideas about how these materials might be used, it is important to highlight that any task or stimulus can be used in dynamic assessment. The three essential elements outlined earlier in Chapter 1 are what make the assessment/intervention work distinctly as *dynamic* assessment, rather than the specific nature of the content, and that counts even if you are only having dialogue with the child or young person about their learning. Here is a reminder about the three essential elements of dynamic assessment:

1. There is a collaborative nature to the assessment/intervention context, based on the Vygotskian notion that we can learn just as much, if not more, about a child's cognitive development, and how they learn, by working with them, together, rather than assessing what they can do on their own.
2. There is a flexible nature to the assessment/intervention, whereby we do not need to stick to rigid procedures or scripts. As assessors, if we wish to take a different direction during the assessment/intervention because we think it will be more productive in terms of exploring the child's learning, then we will.
3. There is a focus on emerging cognitive skills (processes) rather than those that are fully developed (products), as well as a focus on the affective or emotional factors of learning.

CHAPTER 5

FEEDFORWARD

Background and rationale

One of the most fundamentally important aspects of dynamic assessment practice is how the information gathered can be fed back to those working with the child, or to the child themselves, so that positive change can be realized in the classroom. It is this aspect that many educational psychologists in the UK have struggled with over the last 25 years since the approach became incorporated into their practice (Deutsch & Reynolds, 2000; Hill, 2015; Stringer, 2018).

Feeding back following dynamic assessment is just as important as feedback that goes on in an everyday classroom. As Miser (2012) argued, feedback from a student's performance should always form the basis of assessment and intervention, *in order to guide future performance*. The onus is on the teacher, or mediator, to provide the student with 'tips on what they can do in the future to improve in areas that need correcting' (p.1).

Jackson *et al.* (2009) discussed the notion of 'effective feedback' and what that should entail. The important aspect is to demonstrate where we are in relationship to objectives that are set, and what we need to do to get there. Below we will outline how essential it is to set goals and describe what is needed to achieve them. Providing feedback clearly and effectively is not only trying to help students to learn, but also to help them get better at learning (Jackson *et al.*, 2009). Extending Jackson's ideas further, it is fundamentally important that children view the dynamic assessment (or any tasks that may be done in the classroom) as 'opportunities to learn and grow, rather than as assaults on their self-concept' (Chaparro, Nese & McIntosh, 2015, p.4).

John Hattie's work on visible learning has effective feedback at its core. As he states:

> The most powerful single moderator that enhances achievement is feedback. The simplest prescription for improving education must be 'dollops of feedback'…providing information on how and why the child understands and misunderstands, and what directions the student must take to improve. (1999, p.9)

We can relate these general ideas of effective feedback in a classroom to how we feed back following dynamic assessment. In our training programme, we often make links between dynamic assessment and formative assessment. Teachers understand and are trained in formative assessment, where a focus is on next steps of learning, rather than on a score, grade or percentage (summative assessment). The purpose of formative assessment is often written as 'to reduce discrepancies between current understanding/performance and a desired goal'

(Hattie & Timperley, 2007, p.86). This discrepancy can be reduced by teachers, who can help students to formulate appropriate, challenging and specific goals, and also by the students themselves, for example through increased effort and the use of more effective strategies. Hattie and Timperley (2007) stated that the three questions that formative assessment is aiming to answer are as follows:

1. Feed-up – where am I going?
2. Feedback – how am I doing?
3. Feedforward – where am I going next?

It is this last concept, that of feeding forward, that encapsulates the work we do with dynamic assessment. Below we will discuss different ways where the information gathered from dynamic assessment can be utilized to draw up a coordinated plan of intervention with the aim of effecting change in the classroom. Or, in other words, how we can feed forward and consider next steps.

The Learning Profile

In *Improving Learning Through Dynamic Assessment* (Lauchlan & Carrigan, 2013), we introduced the idea of the Learning Profile, a working document that could be used both by the adults working with the child, and by the child themselves. We have reproduced the two versions in this textbook – see Chapter 7, Resource 5.1 (Adult Learning Profile) and Resource 5.2 (Children's Learning Profile).

The Learning Profile is designed to quickly summarize the information that has been gathered, but more importantly, outline the strategies that are being put in place to foster the development of the emerging learning principles. The need to have a one-page action plan was apparent to us after several years of writing lengthy reports following dynamic assessment, including several pages of detailed analysis of the Cognitive and Affective Learning Principles displayed by the child, and the child's response to some of the Mediated Learning Principles. We quickly realized that while such information was rich and thorough, the reality was that such an abundance of information was difficult for those working with the child (e.g. class teachers, teaching assistants, learning support teachers, and parents) to translate into important pedagogical changes that would make a difference to the child's learning environment.

Thus, the Learning Profile was suggested as a way to summarize the key points of the dynamic assessment, ideally focusing on only three of the Cognitive and Affective Learning Principles, and the strategies being put in place for each. This is not to deny the importance of a full and lengthy report that may be written to supplement the Learning Profile. In fact, we acknowledge that the expectation of many in education (including parents) after requesting an educational psychologist's involvement is that a report of several pages is produced. The Learning Profile can be an addendum to the report, but ensuring its importance as a positive way forward for the child's learning, and identifying next steps, is emphasized.

We are often asked in training about the decision-making process involved in reducing the information from the dynamic assessment to just three of the Cognitive and Affective Learning Principles. Of course, we recognize that there may be some differences as to which three might be decided on from practitioner to practitioner. However, a general rule to follow, and which represents a faithful interpretation of both Vygotsky (1978) and Feuerstein's (Feuerstein *et al.*, 2002) theories, would be to focus on those learning principles that demonstrate the most change during the course of the assessment, since it is these learning principles that are emerging (located in the Zone of Proximal Development), just under the surface of the child's independent level of performance (or Zone of Actual Development). It is through these more 'modifiable' or 'changeable' learning principles that we can make some important changes in the classroom that will lead to improvements in the child's learning.

While the above interpretation of Vygotsky and Feuerstein's theories would be considered one way to draw up the Learning Profile, another approach would be to focus on a clear strength that the child has displayed from beginning to end of the assessment, and therefore that could be better utilized in the classroom. Thus, the child may not necessarily demonstrate change in this aspect of their learning, but it could be a learning principle that could be encouraged more in the classroom setting. Alternatively, a practitioner may take the view that a child demonstrates acute difficulty in one of the learning principles despite the assessor's attempts to intervene with mediated learning strategies, and therefore it is decided that this particular learning principle requires a level of *intense* intervention in the expectation that such an intervention will make a difference to the child's learning in the classroom. In other words, the dynamic assessment practitioner has to decide on whether to include:

- those learning principles where the child demonstrated change during the assessment, perhaps that were not evident at the beginning of the assessment but were evident by the end (in other words, those that are in the Zone of Proximal Development)
- those learning principles where the child demonstrated clear strength from beginning to end of the assessment (in other words, those that are in the Zone of Actual Development)
- those learning principles where the child did not demonstrate any change and which remained areas of difficulty despite the mediator's attempts to intervene (in other words, those that are in the Zone of Potential Development, or just beyond)
- a mixture of all three kinds of learning principles described above.

We understand that there will be individual differences in how dynamic assessment practitioners will undertake this decision-making process, and while some may argue that this may not necessarily be a positive thing (in terms of lack of consistency in service delivery), there are three points we can make in relation to this. The first point is that, even if there are some individual differences, the overarching objective remains the same – to effect positive change through a careful analysis of the learning principles that a child engages in during the assessment and making practical suggestions as to how these changes can be enacted in the classroom. How that positive change comes about is largely irrelevant. The important thing is that change happens and continues to happen as a means of making improvements in the child's learning. The second point is that because a review process should be built into the use of the Learning Profile, it means that when one is updating the Learning Profile after a few months, there is a strong possibility that the learning principles that were not selected for the initial version of the Learning Profile, but might have been by another practitioner, *will* be identified at the first review. Finally, the third point to make is that there are many aspects of educational psychology work, particularly therapeutic work, where there will be differences from practitioner to practitioner, but it doesn't make the work less valuable, less relevant or less important. Dynamic assessment as done by practitioners does not aim to be standardized in the sense that the exact same outcomes would be found from one assessor to the next. A core element of feedforward is to clarify the child's own objectives and help them to set goals.

What are goals?

The study of personal goals and how such goals impact on one's life is regarded as a cornerstone of positive psychology (Locke, 2005). There is also an abundance of information surrounding goal theory and goal constructs (Austin & Vancouver, 1996; Senko & Harackiewicz, 2005). A consistent finding in the literature is the belief that personal goals are important (particularly at school) as they set out targets to aim for and provide standards for evaluating performance (Beale & Crocket, 2013; Green *et al.*, 2012; Litalien *et al.*, 2013; Locke & Latham, 2002; Messersmith & Schulenberg, 2010; Vasalampi, Salmela-aro & Nurmi, 2010; Yeager, Bundick & Johnstone, 2012).

It is agreed that, when pupils set goals for themselves, they act as representations of their future and, if they matter to them and are viewed as realistic and attainable, they will act as strong motivators (Beale & Crocket, 2013; Hofer & Chasiotis, 2003; Vasalampi *et al.*, 2010). Goals for the future help to both structure and energize pupil behaviour (Danish 2002; Vasalampi *et al.*, 2010). Maehr (1984) states that goals refer to how a person defines situational success and failure. The very purpose of working towards goals enhances student wellbeing (Messersmith & Schulenberg, 2010). It is important to differentiate between goal content and goal process. Goal content is defined as the content of a desired state (e.g. to complete high school or to go to university) or a state which is to be avoided (e.g. to get divorced) (Chan *et al.*, 2006). Goal processes include 'behaviours and cognitions associated with these goals such as goal commitment, expected age for goal attainment (temporal extension) and attributions for goal success' (Massey, Gebhart & Garneck, 2008, p.423).

It is clear that goal setting is a vital skill for success in just about anything in life, yet very little attention is given to the process involved in setting effective goals. The acronym SMART (specific, measurable, attainable, relevant and timely) is often referred to when goal setting with adults. While these are helpful in creating a structured framework for the process of planning, they do not capture the personal investment required. Adults are more able to work within an extrinsic process model (e.g. at work), but to create change in children the model requires an element of intrinsic motivation.

Locke and Latham (2002, p.706) maintain that goals serve four primary functions:

1. By specifying a goal, one must direct focus towards that goal and away from activities unrelated to that goal.
2. The setting of a goal is a behaviour-stimulating act. According to Locke, high goals lead to greater effort than low goals.
3. Goals have a positive effect on persistence. However, there is an inverse relationship between time and intensity.
4. Goals subconsciously direct the person toward discovering better ways or physical acts.

DYNAMIC goals (grasping opportunities and learning success)

DYNAMIC goals are goals that create change or action by the learner, scaffolded by the educator. DYNAMIC goals create a bridge from feedback (where they are now) to feedforward (where they want to get to). We recommend collaboration with the child to think DYNAMIC:

Define your goal
Define what is important to the child; allow them to dream big and see their preferred future, perhaps where they are confident to try new things. Identify what learning principles they want to work on and discuss why they are important in achieving their goal. As noted previously, it is helpful to have a degree of flexibility around this, and it does not matter which one they decide to start with, as you will introduce more in subsequent review sessions.

Take control of your goal; ask, 'Is it under Your control?'
'I will be able to achieve my goal if…and I wish the maths exam was easier' are common statements from children. Well, if only we could make the maths exam easier, but that's not a goal – a goal needs to be something that you can do something about. You cannot control how hard a test is, but you can control the work you do for it. Similarly, we cannot control how people act – we can only control ourselves and how we act or respond to others.

No room for negativity
If you are trying to be healthier for example, saying 'I can drink more water' is a better goal than 'I can't drink any more fizzy drinks'. 'I won't be late handing in my homework' is better phrased as 'I will hand my work in on time'. Stating goals in a positive way is much more likely to motivate than when stated negatively. Basically, *positive thoughts, words and actions create positive thoughts, words and actions.* Success comes in 'I can' statements, such as 'I can ask for help'.

Attainable
Feeding forward has to strike a balance between being easy enough to notice small steps of change, and having enough challenge to show developmental progress. Appropriate amounts of mediation should also be noted here. Considering how much scaffolding the child will require for this task should be part of the plan.

Measurable outcomes
How will you know you have made a difference if you don't measure the change? Writing measurable outcomes is a three-step process which involves outlining the desired outcome, the assessment method that will be used and the criteria for success. If the child has an Additional Support Plan, for example a GIRFEC (Getting It Right for Every Child) in Scotland or EHCP (Education, Health and Care Plan) in England, then their DYNAMIC goals should be included within this document. Setting short timescales keeps everyone focused and on track; short reviews or even review check-ins should be no more than six to eight weeks. Check-ins should include people who may notice the change, for example teaching assistants, additional support needs assistants or anyone else identified by the child as part of their 'dynamic team'.

Important to you

When summing up a dynamic feedforward plan, ask the child, 'Is this goal important to you?' If the answer is no or 'My mum wants me to' or 'My teacher said I have to' or 'My friends think I should', there is absolutely no point in setting a goal if it is not important to them, because it will not work. It is vital that they create goals for themselves.

Clear and specific

Often people set themselves good goals but do not add details, so how do we know if they have been achieved? I will start running… When? How far? What for? A specific goal would be more like… 'I am going running on Tuesdays at 6.30pm for 30 minutes or for 5km because I want to improve my fitness.' When your goal is clear it is easier to measure success.

We have designed some resources to help you to formulate DYNAMIC goals with the children and young people with whom you work. These goals can work alongside the Learning Profile, as described above. You can find a full description of each of the resources below, and how to use them, in Chapter 7.

- Resource 5.1: The Learning Profile (Adult Version)
- Resource 5.2: The Learning Profile (Child Version)
- Resource 5.3: The Goal Ladder
- Resource 5.4: Overcoming Barriers
- Resource 5.5: Creating a Dream Team
- Resource 5.6: Rebounding
- Resource 5.7: Identify Your Own Skills and Strengths
- Resource 5.8: Goal Keepers
- Resource 5.9: Goal Busters
- Resource 5.10: My Future
- Resource 5.11: Visualize Your Goal

Summary

In this chapter, we have provided ideas on arguably the most important element of dynamic assessment – how to move forward following the assessment itself. We have discussed the concept of the Learning Profile, both for the adults working with the child, and for the child themselves. This is a quick, easy-to-use resource that can provide a focus for the intervention following the dynamic assessment work. Alternatively, the practitioner may want to spend more time formulating DYNAMIC goals with the child or young person, using the information gathered from the dynamic assessment as a focus for the discussion. Several resources and worksheets have been described above that could be used to help the child develop their DYNAMIC goals. These can be enshrined in the Cognitive and Affective Learning Principles, or they may involve more ambitious, long-term goals too. The resources described above can also help the child or young person reflect on who is around to help them achieve their goals (Creating a Dream Team, and Goal Keepers), as well as the obstacles that may be put in their path (Overcoming Barriers, and Goal Busters).

Part 2

The Dynamic School and Practical Resources

CHAPTER 6

THE DYNAMIC SCHOOL

Dynamic assessment: a whole-school approach

As educational psychologists (EPs), we advocate a contemporary approach to dynamic assessment. In other words, we use dynamic assessment in almost all aspects of our work, not just as part of our assessment process, but also in the language we use during conversations with parents and staff. It also influences our planning and interventions. Over the years, teachers in the schools we have worked with have asked us about the approach and this has led to teachers often observing our dynamic assessment sessions with children. We would use the dynamic assessment learning principles as a framework for these observations and make time for discussion afterwards. These sessions provided the opportunity to discuss not only the ability of the learner, but the complexity of the task, the mediated learning skills used and the competency of the mediator. Teachers were already familiar with the concept of formative assessment and learning and could already see the value in developing the approach across the school. Nevertheless, it is only once an approach is truly accepted, embedded and part of the everyday experience within the school that it will become a developed characteristic of the school ethos.

A Dynamic School understands the importance of the mediator in developing the potential of the learner. It is less concerned with the child's actual performance, but rather the child's Zone of Potential Development. In a Dynamic School, learning and mediation principles are understood and are actively demonstrated. Dynamic assessment should be considered as a cyclical immersive model where the approach permeates all teaching and learning and is considered part of the ethos of the school.

Dynamic assessment has been traditionally used in schools by psychologists or speech and language therapists after a child has been identified with having a learning concern. This approach has been procedural, despite the process being cyclical, and the outcomes are often summative, often only focusing on the cognitive ability of the child with little or no account of the mediation principles required from the educator, or the types of tasks that would be beneficial, linked to the child's Learning Profile. Instead, we began to work with teaching staff on creating a contemporary approach to dynamic assessment, one that would foster a dynamic ethos across the whole school. We started training more and more teachers in the approach and developed training approved by the General Teaching Council, the British Psychological Society and local authority schools. We collaborated with school leaders to develop a process to effectively embed the dynamic assessment approach and create a Dynamic School.

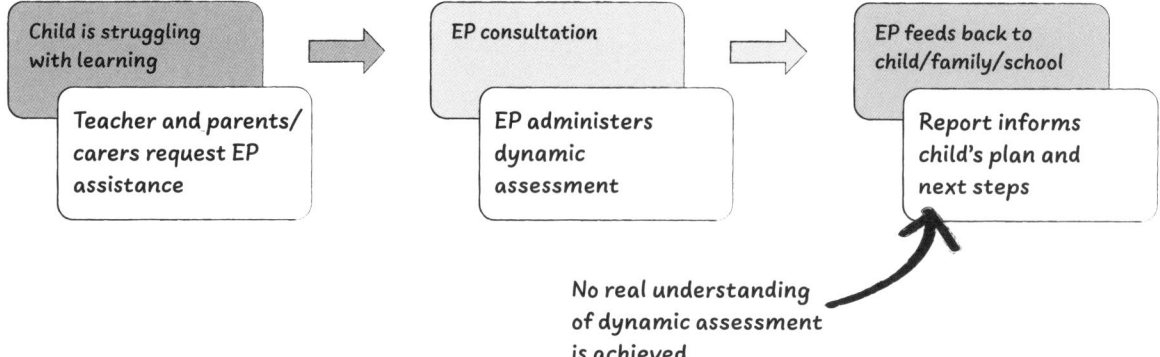

Figure 6.1: Traditional model of dynamic assessment (process driven)

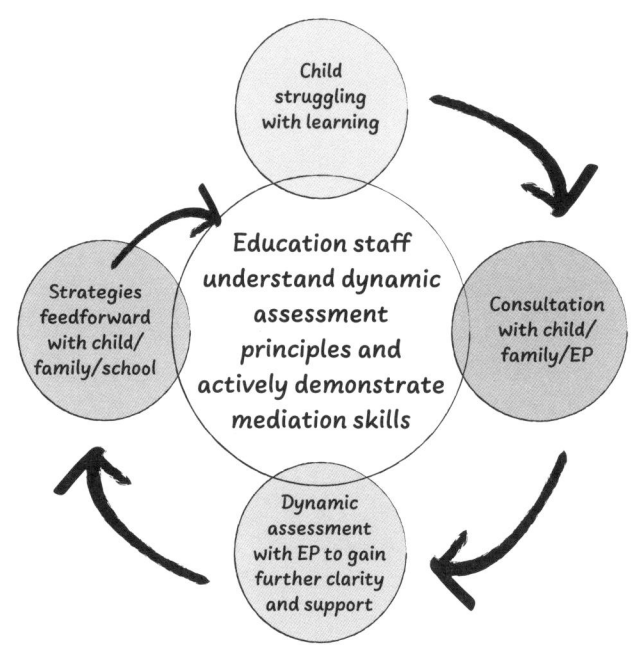

Figure 6.2: Contemporary model of dynamic assessment (immersive)

Creating a dynamic ethos

To create a Dynamic School ethos, one where change is embraced and learners are scaffolded to achieve their learning potential, you need to start with the headteacher. The momentum for change always begins with the school's senior leadership team (SLT). The ideas, however, may not necessarily emerge from the SLT. Good leaders consult with their staff to identify strengths and barriers within their team. To create a sustainable, positive school ethos, the SLT need to create the organizational conditions and shared vision for all stakeholders (staff and students, parents and local community) to buy into. It is this shared vision that is the catalyst for change. School identity can be defined by the culture and ethos which is typically present. Teachers and other education staff embody the ethos of the school by their interactions with the children and are therefore integral to creating lasting change. This includes creating a sense of community among stakeholders in adhering to a projected vision for the school.

Schools with a strong ethos have higher levels of teacher retention, increasing levels of achievement and success and better overall performance. With such potentially powerful results, schools should be encouraged to measure and evaluate their current climate by making explicit their ethos, knowledge, previous training, and beliefs which are embedded in classroom practice. The most effective way to audit the current climate within a school and create a change in whole-school ethos is by adopting an implementation science approach (Fixsen *et al.*, 2015).

Adopting an implementation science approach

Implementation science (IP) provides a framework for effectively embedding evidence-based programmes into educational establishments, by considering the phases required to achieve maximum impact while reducing potential barriers or negative variables.

Each phase of implementation must be thought through carefully rather than delivering training to staff on a new approach, without consultation and a clear purpose. IP makes sure that everyone has the same shared vision and feels personally ready to support change. Our model of dynamic change below is a six-step process that can realistically take two or three years to fully embed.

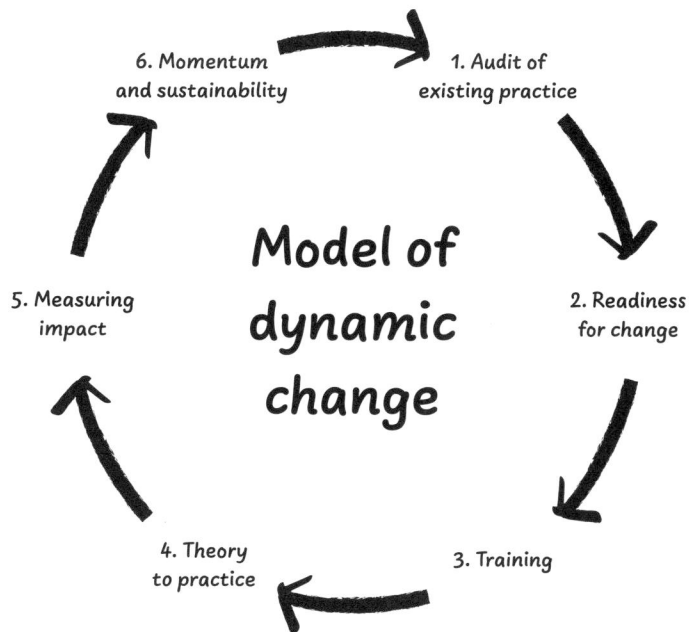

Figure 6.3: Model of dynamic change

> It can be helpful to consider the analogy of painting a home. The more preparation time you spend, the better the overall result. Although jumping in may seem like a quicker way to do the job, things can get messy faster than if you had prepared. You will waste valuable paint (resources) and ultimately take longer to complete the job.

Printable worksheets and checklists to support each phase are included in Chapter 7 (Resources 6.1–6.10).

Phase 1: Are we ready for change?

We all know that sustainable, transformational change does not just happen overnight, there needs to be an agreed implementation plan. Stage 1 of this process is an audit of the existing school practice. Take this opportunity to consider what other educational concepts, theories, training and approaches are already used within your school (Resource 6.1: School Ethos for Learning and Assessment).

Do you really want to make change? If so, this change needs to be recorded in the school's official improvement or development plan so that there is a clear demonstrated commitment from the SLT. Schools are busy places, and even with the best intentions, ideas get lost or under prioritized if they are not part of an actionable plan.

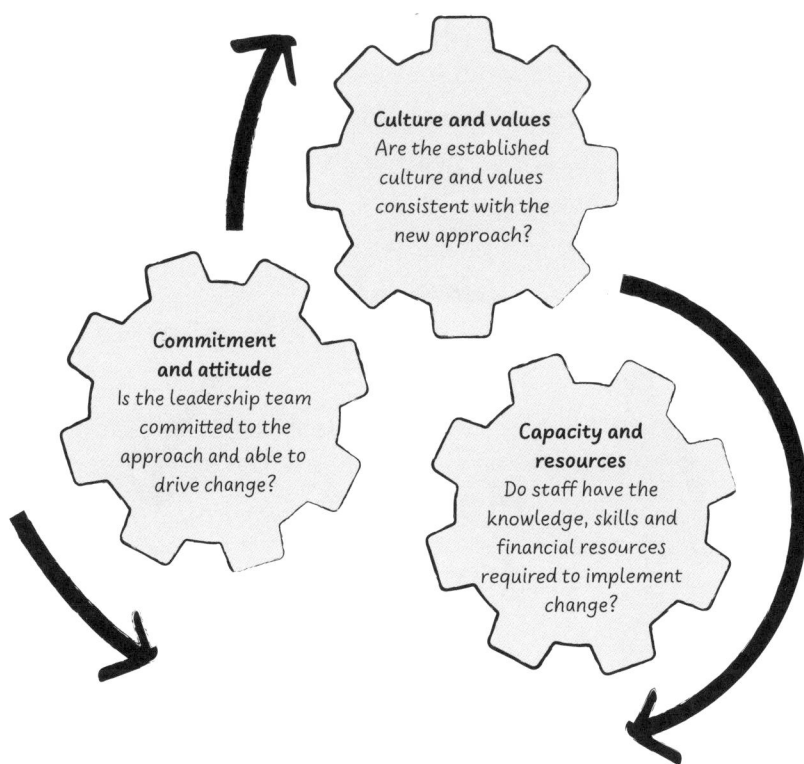

Figure 6.4: The three main drivers of implementation readiness

To fully embed the dynamic ethos across a whole establishment, allocation of time and resources must be considered and carefully planned. For example, what additional time and resources will be available to staff throughout the process? Outcomes and impact must be agreed (see the section 'DYNAMIC goals' in Chapter 5 for help with this), with a view to thinking what this would look like in your school improvement plan and strategic plan. The strategic plan is the logistical bridge between your vision and your plan which breaks down how you are going to achieve your school's vision.

Creating a school vision

School vision and mission statements are important for keeping a school focused on its core purpose. They can also be shared with parents, carers and the wider community to create a shared value system. Workshops that focus on vision and values can give you guiding principles to determine your actions and the words to use in your mission statements. These principles underpin the culture and ethos that drive teaching and learning in schools, and which shape pupil and staff experience. An effective vision should reflect the kind of school you want to create and lead and should be incorporated and visible in every part of everyday school life. You can use Resource 6.2: Vision Exercise for Staff to create your vision.

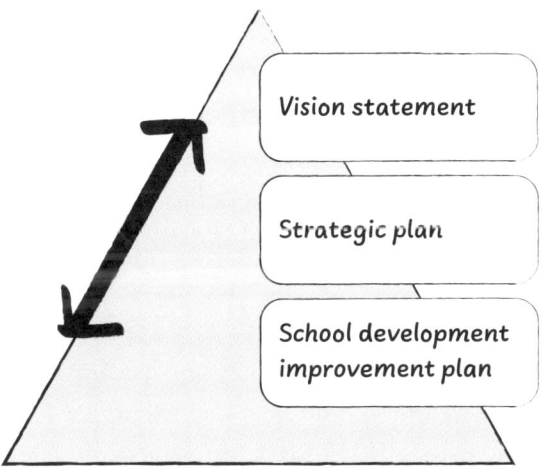

Figure 6.5: Model of dynamic change

Phase 2: Are you and your school ready to be dynamic?

The readiness checklists (Resources 6.3 and 6.4) have been designed to provide a structure for identifying the needs of the school prior to embarking on the project. There is one for the senior leadership team (Resource 6.3) and one for all other staff in the school, including ancillary staff (Resource 6.4). The questionnaire can help with important questions such as: Do the values of the new dynamic assessment approach fit with the shared vision of the school, and if not, what can be done to ensure that they do match? What needs to be done prior to embarking on the implementation stage? Clearly it is important that any potential pitfalls are identified at this stage before implementation, and Resources 6.3 and 6.4 are designed to help with this. More details on how to use the questionnaires are provided in Chapter 7.

Phase 3: How are you going to develop practitioner knowledge and competence?

Teachers are not just starting from scratch, they are familiar with a wide range of related theory and concepts that synthesize effectively with dynamic assessment. A few examples are listed below of some well-known contemporary approaches and theories in teaching and learning. It is not within the scope of this book to go into detail; however, we have provided references for you to easily follow up if you would like to know more about the approaches or theories noted. Our Cognitive and Affective Learning Principles align with these examples, demonstrating that dynamic assessment is complementary, permeating all aspects of learning rather than trying to detract or compete with them. We have been in schools where a certain approach has been selected or adopted and staff then feel they are unable to use another approach. That is certainly not the case with dynamic assessment, as it will seek to enhance existing approaches.

Think about what already underpins your teaching and learning approaches in your school, see how it fits with dynamic assessment and how you can apply this to your teaching and learning strategy. Dynamic Assessment UK (www.dynamicassessmentuk.com) has training sessions suitable for all stages of practitioner, from those who are new to the approach to advanced professionals, underpinned by a coach/mentor model.

Complementary approaches

Visible learning theory

Visible learning means an enhanced role for teachers as they become evaluators of their own teaching. According to John Hattie (2012), visible learning and teaching occurs when teachers see learning through the eyes of students and help them become their own teachers. This allows for more clearly understood communication and interactions and links directly to our 'communication' learning principle and our Mediated Learning Principles. Hattie's aim is for educators to 'know thy impact'. He provides a clear model outlining the most effective and feasible methods to improve learning. Evidence demonstrates that reciprocal teaching and feedback are considered the most valuable classroom approaches, both of which can be developed through dynamic assessment.

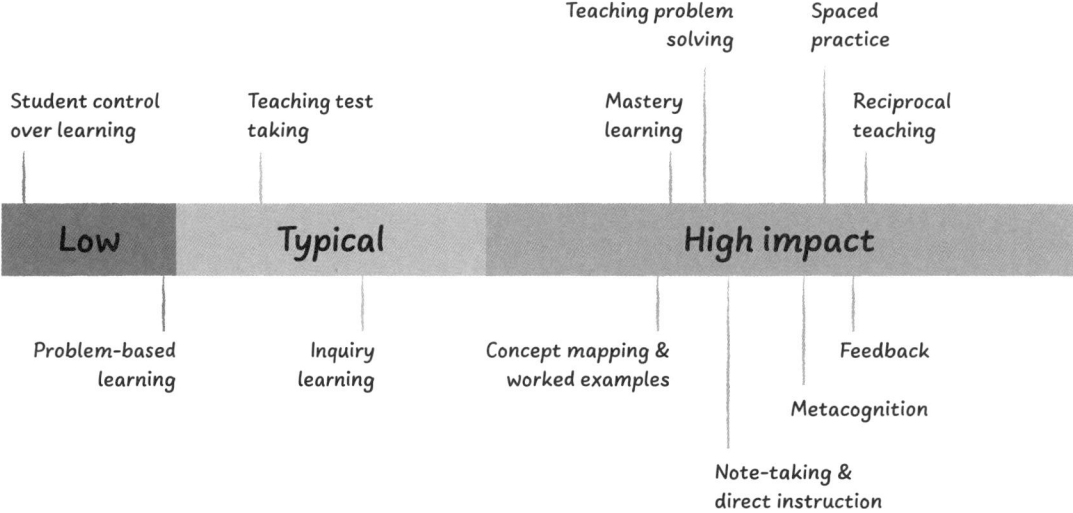

Figure 6.6: Visible learning theory

Executive functions

The ability to compare and contrast is one of the first higher-order reading comprehension skills students are introduced to. And it is no wonder, as the ability to categorize and compare things in terms of their differences and similarities corresponds to some of the earliest stages of cognitive development. Adele Diamond (2013) takes this further with her research on older children and how executive functions make possible mentally playing with ideas; taking the time to think before acting; meeting novel, unanticipated challenges; resisting temptations; and staying focused. Executive functions map directly onto our Cognitive and Affective Learning Principles, as described in Chapter 3 and outlined in Table 3.1.

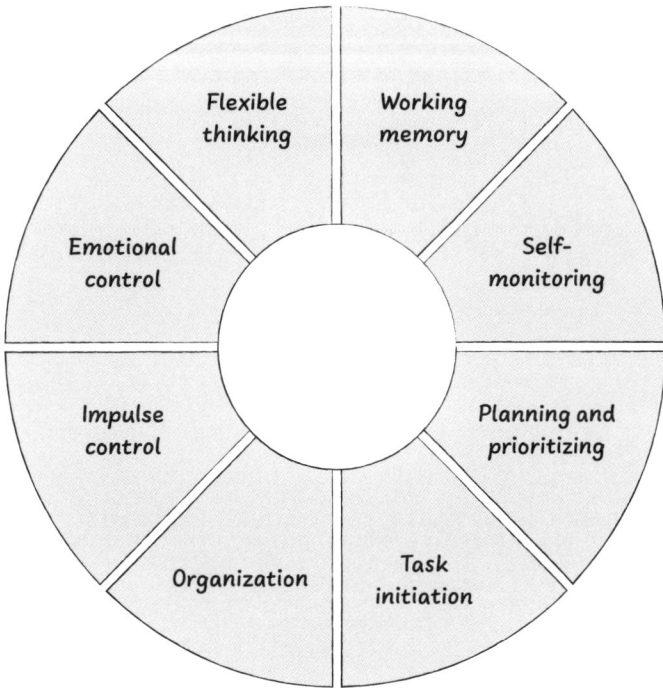

Figure 6.7: Executive functions

Experiential learning

This involves learning from experiences, reflections and actions. For John Dewey (1938), considered the founder of reflective personal learning, reflective learning is an active dynamic process in which one thinks to learn from eventualities of the past or that are happening in the present. This parallels with our focus on reflectiveness, flexible thinking, nature of responses and importance of learner experiences.

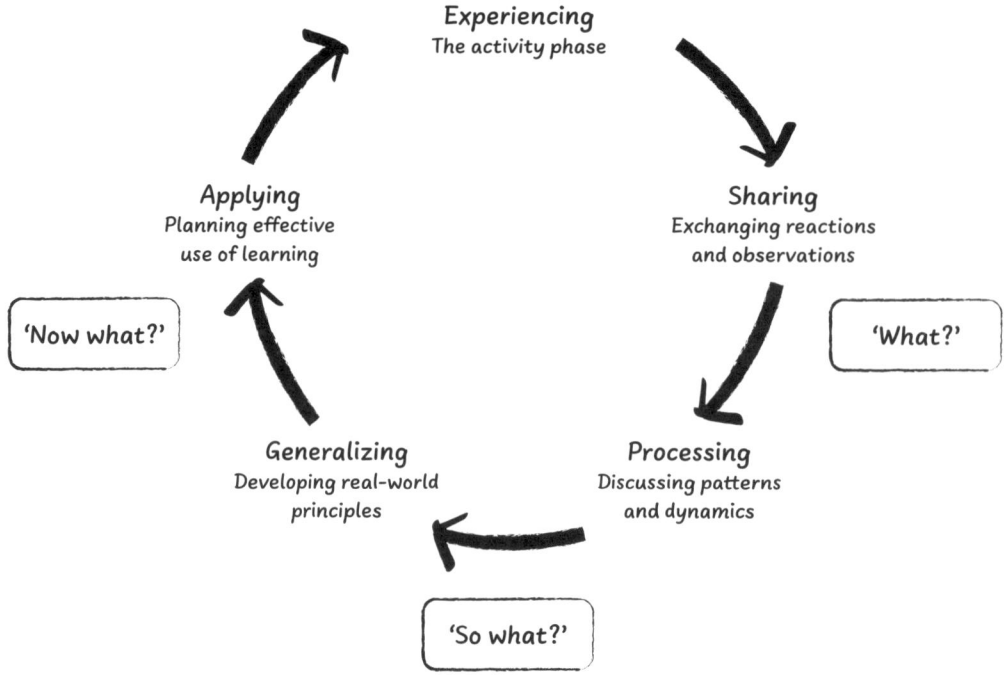

Figure 6.8: The experiential learning cycle

Metacognition

This is a theory based on how people can actively monitor and regulate their own thought processes (Flavell, 1976); in essence, 'thinking about thinking'. We do this when using dynamic assessment by asking questions (mediating the learning) and providing the learner with the tools they need to develop their competence on a task and consider how they might use their newly acquired learning tools to complete other related tasks (in other words, bridging), ultimately becoming independent and autonomous learners.

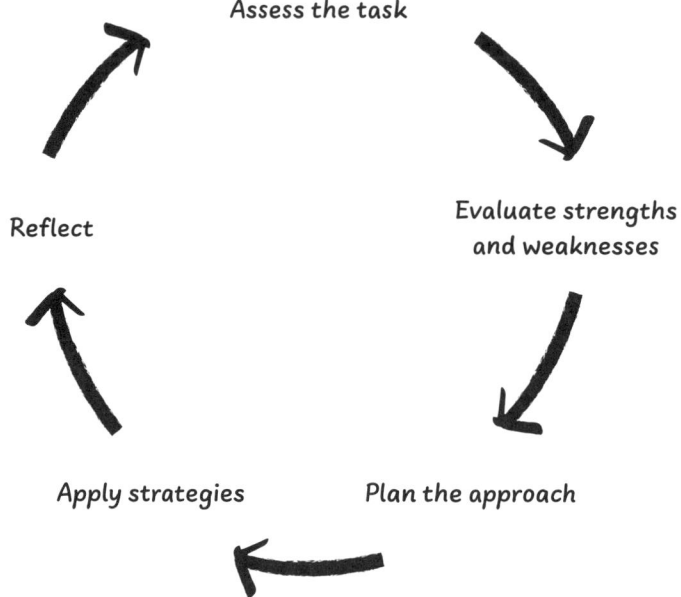

Figure 6.9: The metacognition cycle

The learning pit

This simple idea was created by James Nottingham in 2007 as part of his wider work on meeting learning challenges and taps into the Affective Learning Principles outlined in dynamic assessment. It clearly demonstrates the learner's journey when learning a new concept or trying out a new activity. It is based on ultimately reaching clarity of conceptual understanding (Cognitive Learning Principles) of the task.

Figure 6.10: The learning pit

Spatial orientation

This is one of the key capacities which must develop if a child is to learn to read and write easily. The early childhood movement patterns like rolling, creeping, crawling and rocking, and later walking, running, climbing and swinging, all build a sensory 'map' in the child's brain of where they are in space at any time. In their meta-analysis, Yang *et al.* (2020) suggest effective ways of teaching spatial orientation, which align with dynamic assessment learning and mediation principles.

Mindset

Carole Dweck's seminal work on Mindset (2006), a set of beliefs that shape how you make sense of the world and yourself, suggests that you either have a fixed mindset (ability cannot be changed) or a growth mindset (ability can be developed and learned). Dweck believes that mindset is the psychology of success and that role models are one of the most powerful ways to help people shift their mindset. In dynamic assessment, reaching into the Zone of Proximal Development and aiming to effect change in the learner reflects the same philosophy as believing in a growth mindset. Believing in a growth mindset can have a significant impact on task perseverance and self-belief.

> **SPOTLIGHT ON PRACTICE**
>
> Teaching is a creative profession, not a delivery system. Great teachers do pass on information, but what great teachers also do is coach, mentor, stimulate, provoke and engage. They are the co-creators of change.
>
> **Teacher judgement**
>
> The Covid-19 pandemic magnified the importance and indeed the complexity of 'teacher judgement' when teachers were asked to assess children's learning based on their experience working with the child, as they were unable, due to school closures, to use standard assessment results. Teachers across the UK reported self-doubt and a lack of confidence in justifying their assessments; however, practitioners using dynamic assessment at this time highlighted that this approach offered them a coherent, structured framework on which to base their judgements and therefore increased self-confidence compared to other colleagues.

Phase 4: We can talk the talk, but can we walk the walk?

As we have shown, dynamic assessment is underpinned by a significant wealth of learning theory; nevertheless, *to create change, theory needs to be applied*. For whole-school change to occur, all staff must apply what they have learned – in essence, they must walk the walk.

To create the bridge between theory and practice, we recommend whole-school training on dynamic assessment and mediated learning, followed by three working parties (including as many staff as possible including teaching assistants and janitorial staff). The working parties are each expected to complete an activity workshop based on one of the three sections of the Dynamic Triad. Once complete, they move on to the next section and then the last section so that all groups experience all three section tasks.

The three tasks are:

1. Analysing mediated learning experience in action (Resource 6.6)
2. Identifying and using the learning principles (Resource 6.7)
3. Identifying and reviewing resources (Resource 6.8)

Using video to observe and reflect on dynamic assessment

We have always used video to reflect on dynamic assessment as it can be difficult to observe each aspect of the triad during each session. There are many video-based interventions available to educators, but don't get too hung up on using a specific approach – just a trusty iPad or video camera will do. Resource 6.9 has our top ten tips for using video in schools.

Phase 5: Have we made an impact?

Impact on learners

When measuring impact, we need to return to the reason or objective of the dynamic assessment approach in your school. Rating scales of the Cognitive and Affective Learning Principles – both adult– (Resources 3.3 and 3.4) and child-friendly versions (Resources 3.5 and 3.6) – can be useful tools to evaluate impact on learners.

Impact on educators

A simple and effective way to measure change in mediated learning competency and skills is to administer the Checklist of Mediated Learning Principles before and after dynamic assessment training and practice. This will provide a pre- and post-analysis and pinpoint any potential change in practice (Resource 2.2).

Reflective evaluation using a critical incident technique

Critical incidents (CI) are brief descriptions of vivid memories that a person finds significant during an event, capturing such memories or thoughts by personal reflection (Brookfield, 1996). Brookfield recognized that during every classroom session, pupils and educators experience these moments and that it would be helpful for teachers to know what these are and when they happen. Brookfield then devised a questionnaire which aims to discover the effects of teaching actions on students. He describes the questionnaire as 'a running commentary on the emotional tenor of each class you deal with'.

He postulates that this method of feedback clears up any confusion or ambiguity and allows for any changes to be made before the intervention or teaching programme is complete. It also allows the sessions to be contemporary, within context and to develop by encouraging engagement. Other advantages to CI-based questionnaires include a focus on reflection, room for differentiation of approaches, and the opportunity to build teacher-student trust when students realize that their opinion is valued by the teacher. The questionnaire was designed to be completed by educators or administered to students directly after each class. It comprises five questions, each of which asks participants to write down some detail about events they experienced in class this week (focused on dynamic assessment sessions or interactions). It deliberately avoids asking what they liked or disliked about the session. It instead asks students to focus on specific, more concrete happenings and thoughts.

Five to ten minutes is recommended to complete the questionnaire. There are many advantages of using the CI questionnaire, notably that it allows for some degree of measurement of actual action outcomes and direct effects of the dynamic assessment intervention (Resource 6.10 is an example of a CI-based questionnaire that can be adapted to suit the needs of your class or school).

Phase 6: How do we retain momentum and create sustainability?

Momentum is the elixir of change

Implementing any new approach usually ends with the question 'so what?' How are you going to continue to embed the approach and create lasting change? Training teachers on a new approach may impact on teacher competence and effectiveness for that year, but this is not enough to create lasting change. Staff will require regular training, management and support over a long period of time to sustain performance improvements. To see a significant shift in ethos and behaviours, a sustainability plan will need to be created. This will include improved resources within the school and for the dynamic assessment processes to be accepted as the norm. The dynamic assessment ethos will be visible, adaptive and resilient in the face of new educational demands. According to the diffusion of innovation theory (Rogers, 1962), it takes three to five years in large establishments for new ideas to spread and become embedded. What will the next few years look like in your school? Make sure you log your evaluation and next steps in your school improvement plan to create maximum momentum and long-term impact. Consider how to include the feedforward process (see Chapter 5) as part of the plan. Will you create opportunities for staff peer support through coaching and mentoring? Will you offer regular training and updates? How often? How will you work dynamically with other agencies and initiate a shared culture and language?

> **SPOTLIGHT ON PRACTICE**
> **Recognizing the value of support staff in Thornlie Primary School in North Lanarkshire**
> While completing the readiness checklists (Resources 6.3 and 6.4), school support staff highlighted a few tensions around how the Mediated Learning Principles could be adopted throughout the school day.
>
> 1. They were unsure what was expected of them when they were working individually with a child. They felt that if the child was unable to complete the work independently, they would need to reteach the task otherwise the task would not be complete and this would reflect poorly on the staff member.
> 2. Support staff often finished at 3pm and therefore had very few opportunities to feed back on a child's learning that day.
>
> The issues raised then informed part of a staff focus group to discuss and find suitable solutions. Teachers were able to address this issue by explaining that the teaching assistant was not expected to teach the child and should inform the teacher if the child was unable to do the task. This, however, led to the second point. How can support staff quickly feed back without talking in class (where other children may overhear)?
>
> A facilitated working group was then created to clarify what and how feedback should be communicated by support staff. Their objectives were clear. Feedback needed to be:
>
> - timely (straight after the session)
> - discreet (only for the teacher)
> - time efficient (take the smallest amount of time possible)
> - clear about which mediation principles were used in the session
> - providing actionable next steps for the learner (feedforward).
>
> It was agreed that a fast, discreet and clear method of communication could be in the form of a sticker or stamp in the child's jotter or workbook. The sticker would alert the teacher to the needs of the learner during the session or task (see Resource 6.7 for an example and Table 6.1 for further details).

Table 6.1: Understanding the difference between 'child led', 'adult led' and 'other learning'

	Meaning	Next steps
Child led	The task was easily managed by the child and the staff member was only required to give implicit mediation to complete the task (simple hints and tips).	The child can go on to the next task or challenge set by the teacher and can transfer knowledge gained to other aspects of their learning. However, if the session was child led but then adult led the next day, it could mean the child has not yet consolidated the learning and they may require additional practice on the task.
Adult led	The child was able to complete the task with significant scaffolding by the staff member. Lots of explicit mediation was offered.	If 'adult led' has been highlighted three times consecutively, the teacher may need to go over the lesson or concept with the child again in class or on a one-to-one basis. It is not the job of the teaching assistant to 'teach' the child.
Other learning	The child was unable to complete (or possibly even start) the task. They may require support to co-regulate or focus. They have had lots of mediated support on Affective Learning Principles rather than Cognitive Learning Principles.	The task may be too challenging for the child and/or there may be an additional learning need (cognitive or situational) that needs to be considered. The teacher should initially arrange a quick catch up with the support staff to find out what other learning has taken place, then arrange a one-to-one session with the child to identify or clarify concerns.

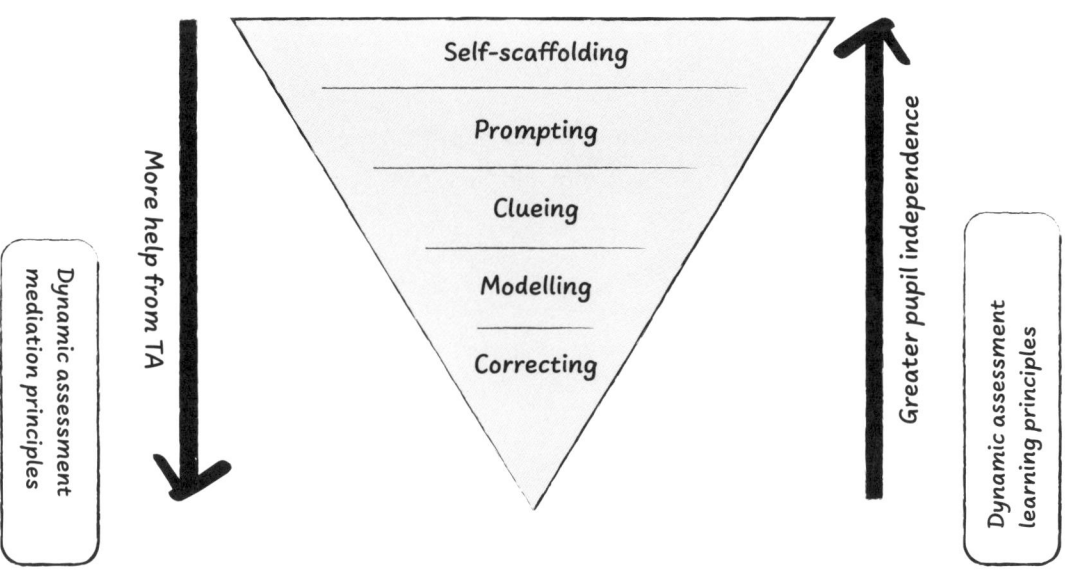

Figure 6.11: EEF model of scaffolding

Feedback can also be used as evidence and planning for personalized children's plans, for example demonstrating frequency and level of support the child has received and the impact on their learning.

The Education Endowment Foundation (EEF) (based on the work of Bosanquet *et al.* (2021)) offers a helpful scaffolding framework for interactions between teaching assistants and pupils (Figure 6.11). It suggests that teaching assistants observe the child's independent performance on the task before they intervene or offer the child support, basically to see how far they can get on their own. This is exactly as we would do in dynamic assessment. This is for teaching assistants to ascertain the amount of challenge the task offers and the level the child is at and to encourage co-operative learning. Our 17 mediation principles (see Chapter 2) develop this model further by demonstrating what this help looks like in practice, while our 24 learning principles offer a framework to understanding the child's ability and level of independence. Table 6.2 synthesizes the EEF scaffolding model with our Mediated Learning Principles based on dynamic assessment theory.

Table 6.2: Links between EEF scaffolding and dynamic assessment mediation principles

	Mediated Learning Principle
Self-scaffolding	Self-regulation Independence
Prompting	Implicit help Bridging Monitoring Scaffolding
Clueing	Encouraging Sharing Challenging
Modelling	Engaging Making sense Self-regulation Planning Positive outlook
Correcting	Explicit help Verbalizing

Creating change

CHAPTER 7

RESOURCES

In this chapter, you will find all the practical resources referred to in the above chapters. These can be photocopied and also downloaded at https://library.jkp.com/redeem using the code UWXGPLG and used to help you develop your practical skills in dynamic assessment.

Resource 2.1: Checklist of Mediated Learning Principles

How to use this resource

1. Have it next to you when doing dynamic assessment as a quick way of recording the Mediated Learning Principles (MLPs) that the child appears to find most valuable when making progress on a task. If this is too difficult to do *while* administering the dynamic assessment, take five to ten minutes as soon as you finish the assessment to reflect on which of the MLPs were most valuable. Ideally, if you have video recorded the dynamic assessment, then you can record this information while watching the play back.
2. Use the checklist to think about developing your own mediated learning style – which MLPs do you use more often than others, which MLPs do you need to work on, which MLPs are difficult to implement, which MLPs come more easily?
3. Ask a colleague to observe your mediated learning and record the MLPs that are being used in the checklist. This can be done to identify the MLPs that are most valuable for the child, but also those MLPs that the adult is engaging in more/less often.
4. Work with a teaching assistant or a support teacher in developing their mediated learning skills, using the checklist as a guide.

Mediated Learning Principles	✓	Comment
Implicit help Is the mediator only having to give small hints, clues and prompts in order to improve performance?		
Explicit help Is the mediator having to give detailed feedback/assistance including explicit discussion of strategies in order to improve performance?		
Engaging Is the mediator trying to engage the child in a reciprocal interaction?		
Making sense Is the mediator promoting meaningfulness in the task?		
Bridging Is the mediator making links to previous or future experiences, e.g. what happens in the classroom?		
Encouraging Is the mediator giving frequent, enthusiastic praise and encouragement in a way that provides valuable feedback to the child?		
Self-regulation Is the mediator trying to ensure that the child slows down, reflects and takes their time?		
Sharing Is the mediator interacting in a way that communicates that they are on the child's side, that they are working together as a team?		
Independence Is the mediator taking a step back at appropriate points to allow the child to take over when working on tasks?		
Planning Is the mediator encouraging planning: showing what to do before beginning to solve the task, and how to set achievable goals?		
Monitoring Is the mediator ensuring that the child is checking their answers?		

Explaining Is the mediator asking for explanations, guiding the child to justify their answers?		
Verbalizing Is the mediator encouraging the child to talk aloud when doing the tasks in order to highlight their thinking?		
Scaffolding Is the mediator gradually building up skills, giving less and less help until the child takes over responsibility for learning?		
Challenging Is the mediator ensuring that tasks are challenging, without overwhelming the child?		
Change Is the mediator highlighting new skills that have been learned and showing the progress that has been made?		
Positive outlook Is the mediator maintaining a positive outlook at all times despite difficulties?		

Resource 2.2: Checklist of Mediated Learning Principles – Rating Scale

How to use this resource

This resource can be used to evaluate your own mediated learning style, or it could be used in collaboration with teaching staff to self-evaluate their own mediated learning skills. For example, the rating scale can help to reflect on which of the MLPs you are currently using more of, and which of them need to be developed further.

Mediated Learning Principles (1=no evidence, 10=lots of evidence)	1	2	3	4	5	6	7	8	9	10
Implicit help Is the mediator only having to give small hints, clues and prompts in order to improve performance?										
Explicit help Is the mediator having to give detailed feedback/assistance including explicit discussion of strategies in order to improve performance?										
Engaging Is the mediator trying to engage the child in a reciprocal interaction?										
Making sense Is the mediator promoting meaningfulness in the task?										
Bridging Is the mediator making links to previous or future experiences, e.g. what happens in the classroom?										
Encouraging Is the mediator giving frequent, enthusiastic praise and encouragement in a way that provides valuable feedback to the child?										
Self-regulation Is the mediator trying to ensure the child slows down, reflects and takes their time?										
Sharing Is the mediator interacting in a way that communicates that they are on the child's side, that they are working together as a team?										
Independence Is the mediator taking a step back at appropriate points to allow the child to take over when working on tasks?										
Planning Is the mediator encouraging planning: showing what to do before beginning to solve the task, and how to set achievable goals?										
Monitoring Is the mediator ensuring that the child is checking their answers?										
Explaining Is the mediator asking for explanations, guiding the child to justify their answers?										
Verbalizing Is the mediator encouraging the child to talk aloud when doing the tasks in order to highlight their thinking?										
Scaffolding Is the mediator gradually building up skills, giving less and less help until the child takes over responsibility for learning?										
Challenging Is the mediator ensuring that tasks are challenging, without overwhelming the child?										
Change Is the mediator highlighting new skills that have been learned and showing the progress that has been made?										
Positive outlook Is the mediator maintaining a positive outlook at all times despite difficulties?										

Resource 2.2 © Fraser Lauchlan and Clare Jones Daly, *Applying Dynamic Assessment in Schools*, 2023

Resource 2.3: Guide to Building Mediated Learning Competencies

How to use this resource

Use this resource to reflect on your own practice and think about whether you are using these skills during your teaching and assessment. You can video your session or alternatively ask someone you trust to observe your practice and see whether there are any areas that can be adapted to help specific children. Please note that 'implicit help' and 'explicit help' have not been included in this resource as they are self-explanatory (see Table 2.1 and Resources 2.1 and 2.2 for more detail).

Mediated Learning Principle	Evidence: what does it look like in practice?	Level of evidence: no evidence (N), some evidence (S), lots of evidence (L). Add notes
Engaging	<ul><li>Is the mediator trying to engage the child in a reciprocal interaction?</li><li>Is the child *fully involved* in the interaction?</li><li>Is the child contributing to the interaction?</li><li>Is the child aware that you are working together (i.e. that it is not too much teacher led)?</li><li>Is the adult working at the child's level of understanding?</li><li>Is the mediator using phrases such as 'What did you like about the task?', 'What did you not like?', 'What did you find easy?', 'What did you find difficult'?</li></ul>	
Making sense	<ul><li>Is the mediator promoting meaningfulness in the task?</li><li>Does the child know why they are doing the task?</li><li>Does the task *make sense* to the child?</li><li>Is the information discussed relevant to the child?</li><li>Is the mediator using phrases such as 'Did you understand everything okay?', 'Do you need to ask any questions'?</li></ul>	
Bridging	<ul><li>Is the mediator making links to previous or future experiences, e.g. what happens in the classroom?</li><li>Is the mediator providing a 'bridge' from the current experience to something that the child can relate to? This could be something from the past, or something in the future.</li><li>Is the mediator trying to make connections between different subjects or even within different topics within the same subject?</li><li>Is the mediator using phrases such as 'How is this similar to something you already know/have done?', 'What do you know about this already?', 'Does this remind you of something you've done before?', 'Do you think this is similar to anything else you've done in class?', 'Does this remind you of anything else, maybe even out of school'?</li></ul>	

cont.

Mediated Learning Principle	Evidence: what does it look like in practice?	Level of evidence: no evidence (N), some evidence (S), lots of evidence (L). Add notes
Encouraging	<ul><li>Is the mediator giving frequent, enthusiastic praise and encouragement?</li><li>Does the feedback highlight what the child is doing well?</li><li>Is the feedback *positive* and *genuine*?</li><li>Is the mediator providing non-verbal encouragement such as positive body language and facial expressions?</li><li>Is the mediator using phrases such as 'Well done. Fantastic. Do you know what I liked about what you did there? You did this, this and this…'?</li></ul>	
Self-regulation	<ul><li>Is the mediator trying to ensure that the child slows down, reflects and takes their time?</li><li>Is the mediator using phrases such as 'Slow down', 'Take your time', 'You know you do it better when you stop and think about it', 'Don't rush', etc.?</li><li>Is the mediator trying to make sure that the child takes over this responsibility, e.g. 'Next time, try and slow down by yourself, rather than me having to tell you'?</li></ul>	
Sharing	<ul><li>Is the mediator interacting in a way that communicates that they are on the child's side, that they are working together as a team?</li><li>Is there non-verbal communication from the mediator that signals that this is a shared experience (e.g. eye contact, smiling to each other, body language that leans towards the child rather than away)?</li><li>Is there a sense that the mediator and the child are 'learning partners' in a shared experience?</li></ul>	

Independence	• Is the mediator sometimes withdrawing or taking a step back in order to allow the child to take over? • Is the mediator being careful not to dominate the learning experience? • Is the mediator giving time for the child to answer, sometimes enduring long silences to allow the child to think?	
Planning	• Is the mediator encouraging planning in the child? • Is the mediator breaking more complex tasks down into smaller parts? • Is the mediator emphasizing the importance of planning generally ('No one plans to fail, they only fail to plan')? • Is the mediator using phrases such as 'What do you have to do first? What will you do next?', 'What is your plan here?', 'Do you know what it is you're trying to achieve?', 'What do you expect to find out?', 'Is there any other way you could do this'?	
Monitoring	• Is the mediator ensuring that the child is checking their answers? • Is the mediator using phrases such as 'Did you check it before telling me what the answer was?', 'How do you know it's correct?', 'Do you need to change your answer or do you think it's okay'?	

cont.

Mediated Learning Principle	Evidence: what does it look like in practice?	Level of evidence: no evidence (N), some evidence (S), lots of evidence (L). Add notes
Explaining	<ul><li>Is the mediator asking for explanations, guiding the child to justify their answers?</li><li>Is the mediator using phrases such as 'Can you tell me how you worked that out?', 'What did you do there? Explain to me', 'Tell me how you know that this is the correct answer'?</li></ul>	
Verbalizing	<ul><li>Is the mediator encouraging the child to talk aloud when doing the tasks in order to highlight their thinking?</li><li>Is the mediator using phrases such as 'This time, tell me what you're doing as you do this one', 'Can you talk aloud what you're thinking as you do it'?</li><li>Is the mediator modelling verbalization for the child in order to show how it is done?</li></ul>	
Scaffolding	<ul><li>Is the mediator gradually building up skills, giving less and less help until the child takes over responsibility for learning?</li><li>Is the mediator interacting in a way whereby it is clear that the child is doing things alone by the end of the interaction that before they needed support with?</li><li>Is the mediator using phrases such as 'This time I'm not going to help you to see if you can manage it on your own', 'Can you try this one on your own and see how you get on? Don't worry – I'm here if you need me but we need to try and get you to work alone. That would be better, right'?</li></ul>	

Challenging	<ul><li>Is the mediator ensuring that tasks are challenging, without overwhelming the child?</li><li>Are the tasks difficult and challenging but not so difficult that the child is becoming frustrated?</li><li>Is the mediator using phrases such as 'Let's try some harder ones now. I think you are ready. We can try the first one or two together', 'That was amazing. Would you like to try more challenging ones now? I'm sure you can do it'?</li><li>After the mediation has finished, is the mediator asking, 'What did you find easy?', 'What did you find difficult'?</li></ul>	
Change	<ul><li>Is the mediator highlighting new skills that have been learned during the mediated learning?</li><li>Is the mediator noticing things that the child can do at the end of the interaction that they were not able to do at the beginning?</li><li>Is the mediator using phrases such as 'What have you learned today?', 'Do you know something now that you didn't know before we started?', 'That was amazing. Do you think you would have been able to do that when we started'?</li></ul>	
Positive outlook	<ul><li>Is the mediator remaining positive at all times despite any difficulties?</li><li>Is the mediator being flexible in their approach and trying different ways to make the child understand?</li><li>Is the mediator using phrases such as 'I can see that this approach is not very helpful. Let's try a different way which may be better', 'Come on, I know you can do it', 'Let's try something else which I know you're going to do much better on'?</li></ul>	

Resource 2.3 © Fraser Lauchlan and Clare Jones Daly, *Applying Dynamic Assessment in Schools*, 2023

Resource 3.1: Checklist of Cognitive Learning Principles

How to use this resource

This resource has the list of Cognitive Learning Principles written in the first column and defined as a question for the mediator/assessor/observer. In the next columns, the mediator/assessor/observer can write whether there is evidence of this learning principle (Yes), no or little evidence of this learning principle (No), or whether there is evidence of a change in the adoption of this learning principle by the child or young person as a result of the mediated learning provided (Change). In the final column, there is a space where the mediator/assessor/observer can write notes about each of the learning principles to help with the recording of relevant information for feedback.

Cognitive Learning Principles	Yes	No	Change	Comment
Communication Is the child communicating their answers in a clear and coherent manner?				
Comparative behaviour Is the child comparing objects, noticing what is similar/different?				
Efficiency Is the child working at a reasonable pace rather than taking excessive time to ensure the answer is correct?				
Exploratory behaviour Is the child searching for solutions rather than settling on the first one that comes to mind?				
Justification of response Is the child able to justify their responses, i.e. explain how they solved the problem?				
Memory Is the child able to remember information/strategies sufficiently, in order to complete tasks?				
Nature of response Is the child answering with meaning rather than guessing randomly?				

cont.

Cognitive Learning Principles	Yes	No	Change	Comment
Planning Is the child using a plan or strategy to solve the problem?				
Problem definition Is the child showing that they understand the nature of the task?				
Recognition Is the child able to recognize when answers are incorrect?				
Reflectiveness Is the child pausing to reflect on their answers?				
Spatial orientation Is the child aware of positioning, left and right and coordination?				
Transfer of learning Is the child able to transfer the learning from one problem to the next?				
Vocabulary Is the child labelling the information using the appropriate vocabulary?				

Resource 3.2: Checklist of Affective Learning Principles

How to use this resource

This resource has the list of Affective Learning Principles written in the first column and defined as a question for the mediator/assessor/observer. In the next columns, the mediator/assessor/observer can write whether there is evidence of this learning principle (Yes), no or little evidence of this learning principle (No), or whether there is evidence of a change in the adoption of this learning principle as a result of the mediated learning provided (Change). In the final column, there is a space where the mediator/assessor/observer can write notes about each of the learning principles to help with the recording of relevant information for feedback.

Affective Learning Principles	Yes	No	Change	Comment
Accessible to assistance Is the child seeking help, prompting assistance and willing to become involved in a collaborative exchange?				
Attention Is the child able to sustain attention for a significant period of time?				
Concentration Is the child able to focus and remain concentrated on the task?				
Confidence in correct responses Is the child answering with conviction, sticking to their answers when challenged?				
Flexibility Is the child flexible in their use of strategies and in their general way of working, e.g. are they able to change how they approach a problem?				

Frustration tolerance Is the child attempting problems/tasks regardless of perceived difficulty, e.g. are they keen to try?				
Motivation Is the child keen to perform well?				
Presentation Is the child relaxed/comfortable?				
Task perseverance Is the child continuing to work on the task despite encountering difficulties?				
Vitality and awareness Is the child eager, full of energy and alert?				

Resource 3.3: Rating Scale of Cognitive Learning Principles (Adult Version)

How to use this resource

This resource can be used by those who work with the child to provide a rating from 1 to 10 for each of the learning principles. Thus, the list of Cognitive Learning Principles is written in the first column, defined as a question for the teacher/classroom assistant/parent/adult, and in the rest of the columns the teacher/classroom assistant/parent/adult can provide a rating from 1 (little or no evidence) to 10 (strong evidence) for each of the learning principles. This could be used as a way of gathering evidence of progress in each of the areas of the learning principles, by evaluating over time the ratings provided. Alternatively, the rating scale can be used to stimulate discussion about how to move up the scale on some of the areas outlined; for example, 'What would need to happen for us to move up by 1 (or move up to 10) on the scale for Planning?'

Cognitive Learning Principles (1=no evidence, 10=lots of evidence)	1	2	3	4	5	6	7	8	9	10
Communication Is the child communicating their answers in a clear and coherent manner?										
Comparative behaviour Is the child comparing objects, noticing what is similar/different?										
Efficiency Is the child working at a reasonable pace rather than taking excessive time to ensure the answer is correct?										
Exploratory behaviour Is the child searching for solutions rather than settling on the first one that comes to mind?										
Justification of response Is the child able to justify their responses, i.e. explain how they solved the problem?										
Memory Is the child able to remember information/strategies sufficiently, in order to complete tasks?										
Nature of response Is the child answering with meaning rather than guessing randomly?										
Planning Is the child using a plan or strategy to solve the problem?										
Problem definition Is the child showing that they understand the nature of the task?										
Recognition Is the child able to recognize when answers are incorrect?										
Reflectiveness Is the child pausing to reflect on their answers?										
Spatial orientation Is the child aware of positioning, left and right and coordination?										
Transfer of learning Is the child able to transfer the learning from one problem to the next?										
Vocabulary Is the child labelling the information using the appropriate vocabulary?										

Resource 3.3 © Fraser Lauchlan and Clare Jones Daly, *Applying Dynamic Assessment in Schools*, 2023

Resource 3.4: Rating Scale of Affective Learning Principles (Adult Version)

How to use this resource

This resource can be used by those who work with the child to provide a rating from 1 to 10 for each of the learning principles. Thus, the list of Affective Learning Principles is written in the first column, defined as a question for the teacher/classroom assistant/parent/adult, and in the rest of the columns the teacher/classroom assistant/parent/adult can provide a rating from 1 (little or no evidence) to 10 (strong evidence) for each of the learning principles. This could be used as a way of gathering evidence of progress in each of the areas of the learning principles, by evaluating over time the ratings provided. Alternatively, as described above, the rating scale can be used to stimulate discussion about how to move up the scale on some of the areas outlined; for example, 'What would need to happen for us to move up by 1 (or move up to 10) on the scale for Motivation?'

Affective Learning Principles (1=no evidence, 10=lots of evidence)	1	2	3	4	5	6	7	8	9	10
Accessible to assistance Is the child seeking help, prompting assistance and willing to become involved in a collaborative exchange?										
Attention Is the child able to sustain attention for a significant period of time?										
Concentration Is the child able to focus and remain concentrated on the task?										
Confidence in correct responses Is the child answering with conviction, sticking to their answers when challenged?										
Flexibility Is the child flexible in their use of strategies and in their general way of working, e.g. are they able to change how they approach a problem?										
Frustration tolerance Is the child attempting problems/tasks regardless of perceived difficulty, e.g. are they keen to try?										
Motivation Is the child keen to perform well?										
Presentation Is the child relaxed/comfortable?										
Task perseverance Is the child continuing to work on the task despite encountering difficulties?										
Vitality and awareness Is the child eager, full of energy and alert?										

Resource 3.5: Rating Scale of Cognitive Learning Principles (Child-friendly Version)

How to use this resource

This resource can be used by the children themselves to provide a self-rating from 1 to 10 for each of the learning principles. Thus, the list of Cognitive Learning Principles is written in the first column, defined in child-friendly language, and in the rest of the columns the child can provide a self-rating from 1 (something I do rarely) to 10 (something I do often) for each of the learning principles. This could be used as a way of gathering evidence of progress in each of the areas of the learning principles, by evaluating over time the ratings provided. Alternatively, the rating scale can be used to stimulate discussion about how to move up the scale on some of the areas outlined; for example, 'What would need to happen for us to move up by 1 (or move up to 10) on the scale for Reflectiveness?'

Cognitive Learning Principles (1=I do this rarely, 10=I do this a lot)	1	2	3	4	5	6	7	8	9	10
I communicate my answers in a clear way										
I can spot when things are the same and different										
I work without rushing or taking too long										
I can search for answers to problems										
I can explain how I get my answers										
I can remember information that will help me with my work										
I can choose my answers carefully										
I am able to plan my steps to solve a problem										
I can understand what I am being asked to do										
I notice when my answers are not correct										
I take time to think about my answers										
I can understand positions and know my left and right										
I can use what I have learned to help me with other tasks										
I use the correct words when naming things										

Resource 3.6: Rating Scale of Affective Learning Principles (Child-friendly Version)

How to use this resource

This resource can be used by the children themselves to provide a self-rating from 1 to 10 for each of the learning principles. Thus, the list of Affective Learning Principles is written in the first column, defined in child-friendly language, and in the rest of the columns, the child can provide a self-rating from 1 (something I do rarely) to 10 (something I do often) for each of the learning principles. This could be used as a way of gathering evidence of progress in each of the areas of the learning principles, by evaluating over time the ratings provided. Alternatively, as described above, the rating scale can be used to stimulate discussion about how to move up the scale on some of the areas outlined; for example, 'What would need to happen for us to move up by 1 (or move up to 10) on the scale for Vitality and Awareness?'

Affective Learning Principles (1=I do this rarely, 10=I do this a lot)	1	2	3	4	5	6	7	8	9	10
I can ask for help when I need it										
I can keep my mind on my work and not be distracted										
I can stay interested in tasks										
I can stick to my answers when challenged										
I can change the way in which I try to solve a problem										
I give my work a try even when it looks difficult										
I want to do well in school tasks										
I feel relaxed/comfortable when I'm learning										
I keep going with my work even if it's difficult										
I am awake and ready to learn										

Memory Challenge: How to use these resources (4.1, 4.2 and 4.3)

Cognitive Learning Principles assessed: principally Memory, but also Communication, Comparative behaviour, Nature of response, Planning, Problem definition, Recognition, Reflectiveness, Transfer of learning, Vocabulary.

Affective Learning Principles assessed: Accessible to assistance, Attention, Concentration, Confidence in correct responses, Flexibility, Frustration tolerance, Motivation, Presentation, Task perseverance, Vitality and awareness.

In 'Memory Challenge', the children are asked to view for one minute either 12 (younger children) or 20 (older children) objects that are placed on a tray. After one further minute, where the objects are covered with a tablecloth or towel, they are asked to memorize as many objects as they can using Resources 4.1 and 4.2. Resource 4.1 has space for the task to be used involving 12 objects, and Resource 4.2 for 20 objects. The children can write the objects down on the worksheet, or draw them, or they can name them out loud. The children can be told that they will be asked to recall the objects prior to viewing them. Please see Resource 4.3 for a list of suggested items that you could use for this activity, but anything at all could be used. This activity is designed to dynamically assess the children's short-term memory skills in a fun way. For the mediated learning, different strategies can be discussed with the child; for example:

1. *Picture it!* When you are asked to remember something, try picturing it in your mind. In other words, create a picture of the scene involving the thing you have to remember. The sillier the scene, the better – you are more likely to remember it.
2. *Link it!* You can use linking when you want to remember more than one thing. The basic idea is that you create a connection between the two or more things that you are asked to remember. For example, you are asked to remember a yogurt and a banana. A connection can be created by imagining the banana being sliced into the yogurt to make it more scrumptious.
3. *Position it!* It may help to remember things by connecting them to specific places – this is similar to the 'Link it!' method described above. For example, to remember a watch you can think of it being placed on someone's wrist, or to remember a jotter you could think of it being placed on a school desk. So it is the complete image (watch on wrist, jotter on desk) that you recall rather than the individual items.
4. *Chunk it!* In this method of remembering things, you can cut down a long list of things into smaller parts. For example, if you have to remember a banana, an apple, an apricot and a pear, then rather than trying to remember all of these individually, you can instead chunk these together as remembering that there are four fruits.

Resource 4.1: Memory Challenge Worksheet (Basic)

Can you remember what you saw?

1.	2.	3.
4.	5.	6.
7.	8.	9.
10.	11.	12.

Resource 4.2: Memory Challenge Worksheet (Advanced)

Can you remember what you saw?

1.	2.	3.	4.	5.
6.	7.	8.	9.	10.
11.	12.	13.	14.	15.
16.	17.	18.	19.	20.

Resource 4.3: Memory Challenge: Ideas for Objects to Use

Some ideas for objects to use for a Memory Challenge.

Rubber	Stapler
Pencil	Sellotape
Sharpener	Paintbrush
Marble	Chalk
Coin	Sweet
Scissors	Hairbrush
Ruler	Duster
Watch	Jotter
Button	Toothbrush
Piece of string	Glue stick

Can You Colour?: How to use these resources (4.4, 4.5 and 4.6)

Cognitive Learning Principles assessed: principally Memory, but also Communication, Comparative behaviour, Nature of response, Planning, Problem definition, Recognition, Reflectiveness, Transfer of learning, Vocabulary.

Affective Learning Principles assessed: Accessible to assistance, Attention, Concentration, Confidence in correct responses, Flexibility, Frustration tolerance, Motivation, Presentation, Task perseverance, Vitality and awareness.

In this activity, children are read aloud a set of colours and they are asked to memorize the list in the correct order by colouring in the worksheet provided. The worksheet used will depend on the different age and stage of the child completing the task. Resource 4.4 involves remembering three colours, Resource 4.5 involves remembering five colours, and Resource 4.6 involves remembering nine colours. Space is provided for repeating the task ten times, with different colours used each time. The children are asked to wait to hear the full list before beginning to choose the appropriate coloured pencils or pens. The children can work up from the three-colour worksheet to the five-colour worksheet until they are able to complete the nine-colour worksheet, developing their memory skills throughout the process. Mediated learning can be provided by talking over specific strategies. ('Maybe it will help you to think of an object that is typically these colours rather than trying to only remember the colour itself. For example, you could think of the sky for blue, a tomato for red and a daffodil for yellow, or can you tell me what reminds you of these colours?')

This task can be adapted to a similar activity entitled 'Can You Draw?'. In this activity, children are asked to draw a number of objects that are read aloud to them. For example, 'Can you draw a pencil, a house and a car?' The child then has to draw the three objects in the correct order. The worksheets provided in Resources 4.4, 4.5 and 4.6 can be used if desired, or blank paper can also be used. As with 'Can You Colour?', this activity can be adapted whereby the children have to memorize three, five or nine objects to draw, depending on the age and stage of the children doing the activity. Again, as described above, the child can work upwards from the three objects to the five until they reach the nine-objects worksheet. Alternative ways of doing the same activity but in a different way could be: 'Can You Make?' (e.g. involving play dough whereby the children have to sculpt the number of objects in the correct order: 'Can you make a ball, a sausage and an arch?') and 'Can You Act?' (e.g. where the children are asked to act out a number of actions in the correct order: 'Can you act digging a hole, going to sleep and playing at tennis?').

Resource 4.4: Can You Colour? Worksheet (Three Colours)

Can you colour?

1.			
2.			
3.			
4.			
5.			
6.			
7.			
8.			
9.			
10.			

Resource 4.5: Can You Colour? Worksheet (Five Colours)

Can you colour?

1.					
2.					
3.					
4.					
5.					
6.					
7.					
8.					
9.					
10.					

Resource 4.6: Can You Colour? Worksheet (Nine Colours)

Can you colour?

1.									
2.									
3.									
4.									
5.									
6.									
7.									
8.									
9.									
10.									

Picture Sequencing: How to use these resources (4.7, 4.8, 4.9 and 4.10)

Cognitive Learning Principles assessed: principally Planning and reflectiveness, but also Communication, Comparative behaviour, Nature of response, Problem definition, Recognition, Transfer of learning, Vocabulary.

Affective Learning Principles assessed: Accessible to assistance, Attention, Concentration, Confidence in correct responses, Flexibility, Frustration tolerance, Motivation, Presentation, Task perseverance, Vitality and awareness.

In 'Picture Sequencing', the child is asked to think of an event (e.g. 'Getting ready for school', 'Travelling to school', 'What I did at the weekend', or 'What I did on holiday'). They are then asked to draw a representation of each part of the sequence on the worksheet (see Resources 4.7, 4.8, 4.9 and 4.10 where the task begins with a simpler version with just three steps (4.7), building up to a more complex version involving six steps (4.10)). Alternatively, the child can write on the boxes provided, or their responses can be transcribed by the adult. Four versions are provided to reflect the age and stage of the child; thus the more boxes, the more complex the activity will be. Or the task can be done using all the versions provided here, beginning with the simpler worksheet and working up to the more complex version.

Other variations of the task could include 'When I do my homework', 'What happens at dinner time', 'Getting ready for bed', and so on. Mediated learning can be provided by assisting the child in the steps that they go through in each of these events; for example, 'What happens first when you do this?', 'What happens next?', 'Would you be doing that at this point, or would there be a step before this?', 'How do you know when the activity is finished?'

Resource 4.7: Picture Sequencing – Level 1 (Three Boxes)

Getting ready for school

Name: ....

Age: ....

1.

2.

3.

Resource 4.8: Picture Sequencing – Level 2A (Four Boxes)

Travelling to school

Name: ....

Age: ....

1.

2.

3.

4.

Resource 4.9: Picture Sequencing – Level 2B (Four Boxes)

My weekend

Name: ....

Age: ....

1.

2.

3.

4.

Resource 4.10: Picture Sequencing – Level 3 (Six Boxes)

My holiday

Name: ....

Age: ....

1.

2.

3.

4.

5.

6.

Word Bingo: How to use these resources (4.11 and 4.12)

Cognitive Learning Principles assessed: principally Communication and vocabulary, but also Comparative behaviour, Memory, Nature of response, Problem definition, Recognition, Reflectiveness, Transfer of learning.

Affective Learning Principles assessed: Accessible to assistance, Attention, Concentration, Confidence in correct responses, Flexibility, Frustration tolerance, Motivation, Presentation, Task perseverance, Vitality and awareness.

'Word Bingo' is similar to traditional bingo, but words are used rather than numbers, and instead of calling out the words, the mediator reads out a definition. This task can be helpful in assessing the language skills of a child in a fun way. Resources 4.11 (basic version) and 4.12 (advanced version) provide some ideas as to how this activity can be carried out. The worksheets can be adapted to make up different 'bingo cards'. The number of 'words' needed to complete the game can be flexible, but it is suggested to start with completing a row or a column or a diagonal line (four words), and build up from there to completing the whole worksheet. The task can be made more complicated by reversing the roles, whereby the child has to think up the definitions of the various items, and the mediator can cross them off the worksheet. Mediated learning can include the provision of strategies to try and have the child complete the task systematically ('Look carefully at the first row and see if anything matches what I've described firstly by looking at colour', 'If there's nothing there then go to the second row', and so on. 'Once you've identified the description that matches the colour, think about something else that was said in the description, for example the shape of the object'). Children may find it difficult to keep in their mind the description and scan the worksheet at the same time. Ask them to say out loud what they're thinking about as it will help them to remember. For example, 'Tell me what you're thinking about just after I read the description. What kind of thing do you think it might be? A kind of food, a kind of transport, a kind of animal, a type of sport?' This way you are using chunking methods as described above under the memory tasks Memory Challenge and Can You Colour?.

Resource 4.11: Word Bingo Worksheet (Basic – Answers)

Apple	Banana	Carrot	Peas
Car	Bus	Plane	Train
Cat	Dog	Cow	House
Tree	Ball	Teddy	Hat

Resource 4.11: Word Bingo Worksheet (Basic – Definitions)

Round fruit that can be red or green	Yellow fruit that is long and bendy	Long and pointy orange vegetable that can help you see in the dark	Small green, round vegetable that can sometimes get mushy
Has four wheels, comes in different colours, can be kept in a garage	Has wheels, a driver and can take you to school, sometimes comes as a double decker	Flies in the sky and is driven by a pilot	Goes choo choo and moves along tracks
Has whiskers, purrs and drinks milk	Has four legs and barks and can be a pet	Lives on a farm, goes moo, gives milk	You live in one, has door, windows and maybe a garden
Has leaves, you find it in a forest	Round, you can kick or bounce it	Furry, you can take it to bed and it is cuddly	Wear it on your head to keep you warm

Resource 4.12: Word Bingo Worksheet (Advanced – Answers)

Lorry	Pineapple	Strawberry	Grape
Zebra	Boat	Helicopter	Bike
Giraffe	Elephant	Square	Triangle
Pyjamas	Football	Tennis	Rugby

Resource 4.12: Word Bingo Worksheet (Advanced – Definitions)

A large vehicle that is used to transport goods	A yellow fruit that is jaggy on the outside	A red fruit that you usually eat with cream in the summer	A green fruit that is small, round and juicy
A horse-like animal with black and white stripes	Sails on the sea	Flies in the sky and it has propellers	Has two wheels, a chain, handlebars and sometimes stabilizers
An animal with a long neck and black and yellow stripes	A large animal with a trunk and is either African or Indian	Has four sides of equal length and four right angles	Has three sides and three angles
You wear these clothes at night to go to bed	Sport where the 11 players on each team are trying to score goals by kicking the ball into the net	Sport played with rackets across a net	Sport played with an oval-shaped ball and players can run with the ball in their hands

Resource 4.13: Find Your Way Map

Cognitive Learning Principles assessed: principally Spatial orientation and Vocabulary, but also Communication, Comparative behaviour, Nature of response, Problem definition, Recognition, Reflectiveness, Transfer of learning.

Affective Learning Principles assessed: Accessible to assistance, Attention, Concentration, Confidence in correct responses, Flexibility, Frustration tolerance, Motivation, Presentation, Task perseverance, Vitality and awareness.

How to use this resource

In this activity, the child is asked to provide directions from one landmark to another using a ready-made map. The intention is to assess their positioning and orientation skills in a fun and enjoyable way. The child is asked to provide directions to travel from one place to another on the map; for example, 'If you are in the play park and someone asks you for directions to get to the bank, what would you say?' The task can begin with some simpler directions, for example involving just one element, but can increase in difficulty as the child builds up their feelings of competence. The task involves skills in spatial orientation and perspective taking. Mediated learning can be provided by encouraging the child to break the task down into parts: 'What's the first thing you would need to say?', 'And then, what is the next step?', and so on. 'Do you think it would be a good idea to mention some of the other places that the person has to pass?' How the child approaches the task and overcomes any eventual difficulties can be explored, thus permitting an assessment of the Affective Learning Principles too.

Find Your Way Map

Resource 5.1: The Learning Profile (Adult Version)

How to use this resource

The Learning Profile can be used to summarize quickly and efficiently the conclusions of the dynamic assessment and/or consultation. The three key learning principles will occupy the spaces on the left-hand side of the Profile, and the strategies to foster each of these will be places in the boxes on the right-hand side. This can be completed in collaboration with those working daily with the child or young person, for example the classroom teacher, teaching assistant, and/or the parents. The Learning Profile is intended to be a working document that the adults can refer to during the intervention part of the process, as a reminder of the key aspects of learning that will be targeted. It can be modified and updated as appropriate.

Learning Profile for: ....

Areas that are important for

........................'s learning

Strategies to try out

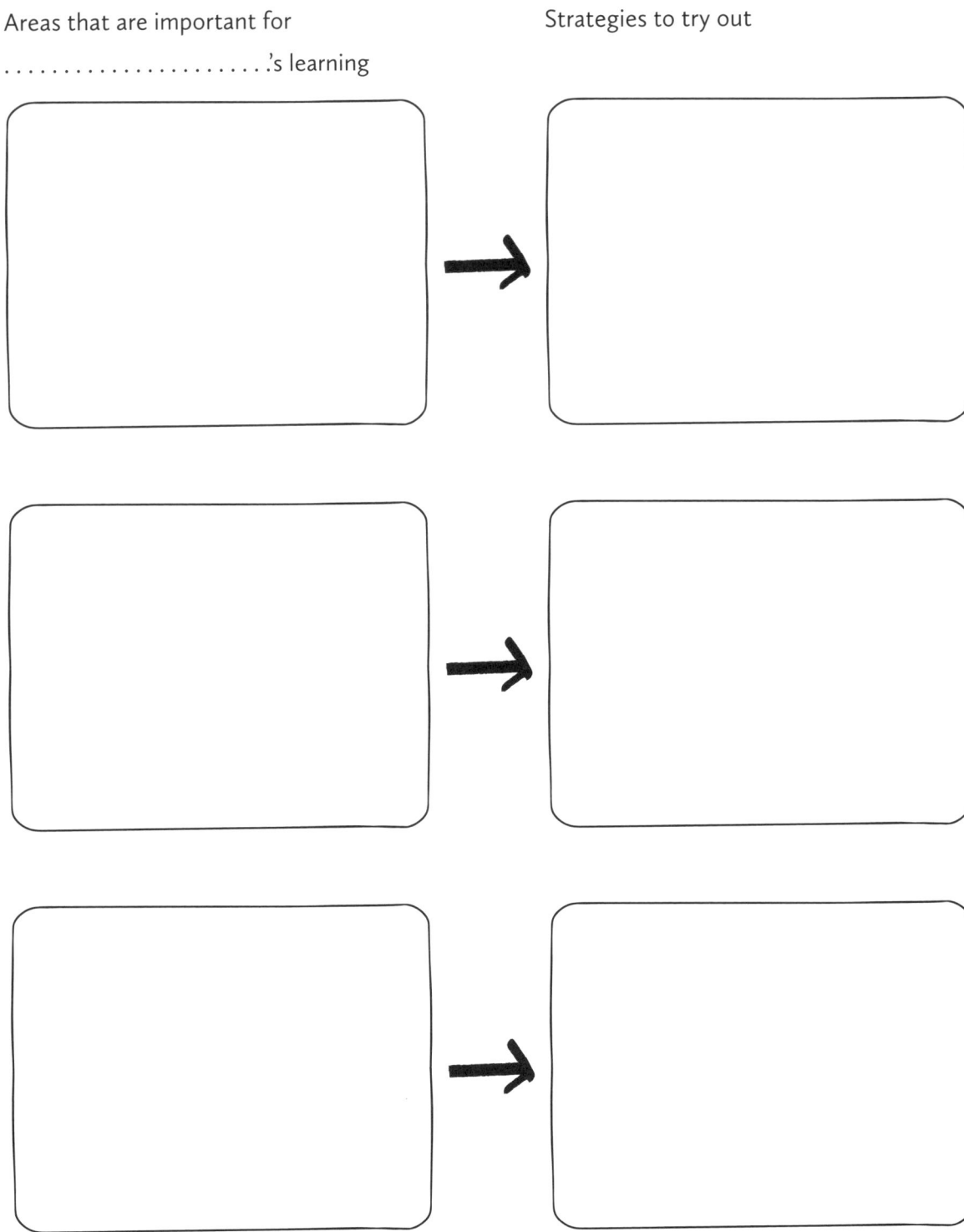

Resource 5.2: The Learning Profile (Child Version)

How to use this resource
This resource should be used in conjunction with the Learning Profile (Adult Version). The three boxes on the left-hand side can be completed with those same learning principles that are written in the adult version, and the 'Things I'm going to work on' can be used to insert some of the activities or strategies that have been suggested to 'cultivate' these learning principles. As with the adult version, the Learning Profile can be updated and modified over time depending on how the intervention process is progressing; for example, by changing some of the learning principles on the left-hand side, or by changing some of the strategies on the right-hand side.

My Learning Profile

Things I did well	Things I'm going to work on

Signed: ....

Date: ....

Resource 5.3: The Goal Ladder

How to use this resource

Part 1: The Goal Ladder (Part 1) is intended to introduce the idea of how to set goals, with a space at the bottom to write the specific goal that the child will be working towards, as well as identifying the success criteria (how will we know when they have reached the goal?). In the context of a dynamic assessment, it might be the case that the child will be working on improving specific Cognitive and Affective Learning Principles. These can be written in the box provided.

Part 2: This resource can be used to break down the goals into four steps: 1) starting off with smaller goals, 2) moving onto bigger goals, 3) stretching the goals further, and 4) the overall vision of what it is the child is moving towards. It is also important to take note of who will notice the child's achievements and celebrate their successes.

Part 3: This resource is the same as Part 2, only the ladder is left blank to be completed by the child or young person. Some of the questions that the child or young person is asked to consider include: 'What step can you do this week?'; 'How will you be able to do this?'; 'Who will notice that you are doing this?'

The Goal Ladder (Part 1)

Visualizing future goals tells us what we want but then we need a plan. One example of a plan is a goal ladder.

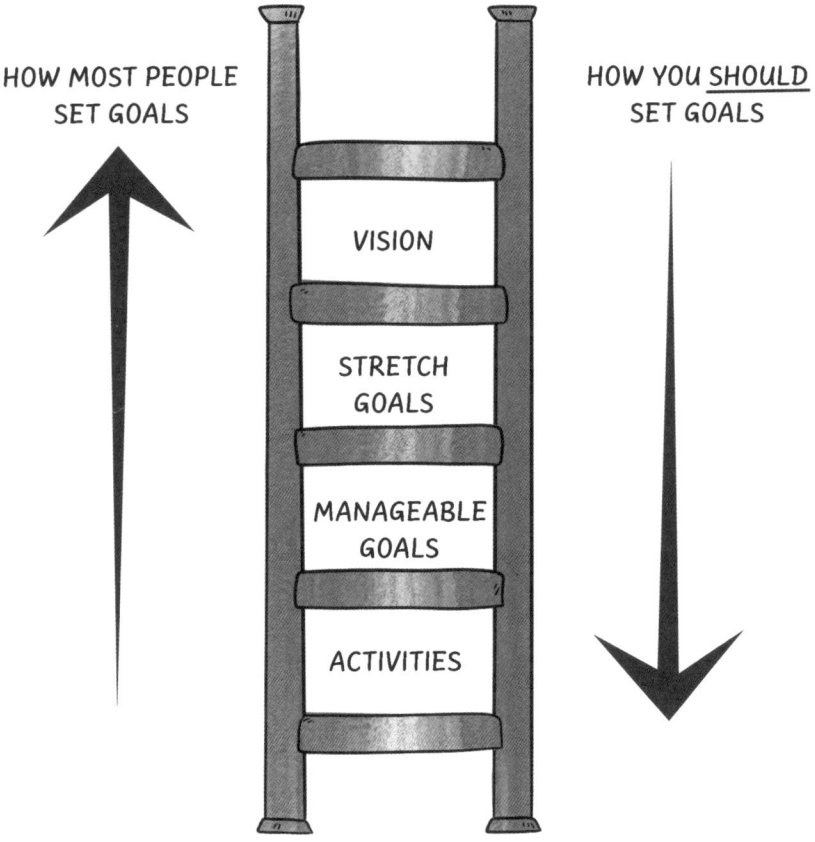

Write your goal here using the success criteria

The Goal Ladder (Part 2)

Break down your goal into four or more steps. *Remember to check the success criteria!*

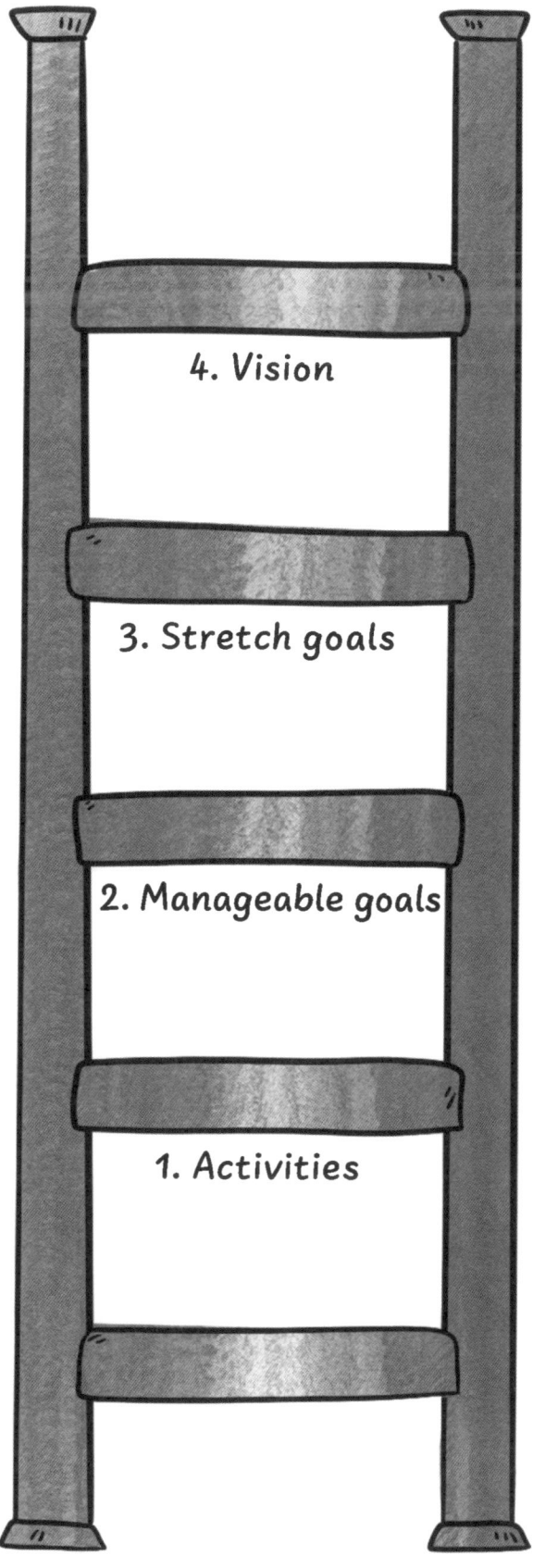

The Goal Ladder (Part 2 – Questions)

What step can you do this week?

....
....
....
....
....
....

How will you be able to do this?

....
....
....
....
....
....

Who will notice that you are doing this?

....
....
....
....
....
....

Now put a target date for when you think you'll achieve each step.

This ladder is only an example, your ladder can have as many rungs as you want. The important part is the questions that accompany the ladder. Write down something that you can do straight-away – things are always easier when you just start. For each thing you list, think about how you are going to do this, *what will you need?* And then think about when you have completed a task, *who will notice your achievement and help you celebrate each task?* Reflecting on the little tasks allows you to make changes to your overall vision.

The Goal Ladder (Part 3)
Break down your goal into four or more steps. *Remember to check the success criteria!*

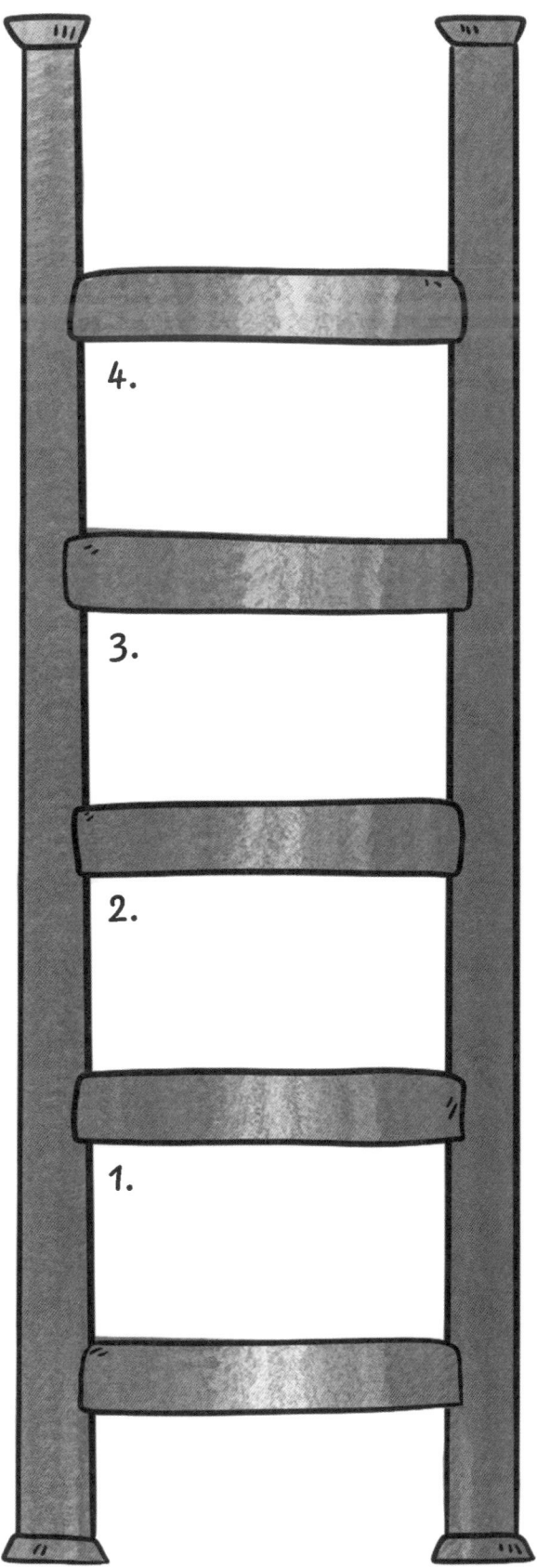

The Goal Ladder (Part 3 – Questions)

What step can you do this week?

....
....
....
....
....
....

How will you be able to do this?

....
....
....
....
....
....

Who will notice that you are doing this?

....
....
....
....
....
....

Now put a target date for when you think you'll achieve each step.

Resource 5.4: Overcoming Barriers

Overcoming Barriers (Part 1)

Creating a goal ladder is a great start but there are often things that get in your way. Things that will make you slip off your ladder. Think of these barriers like *banana skins*.

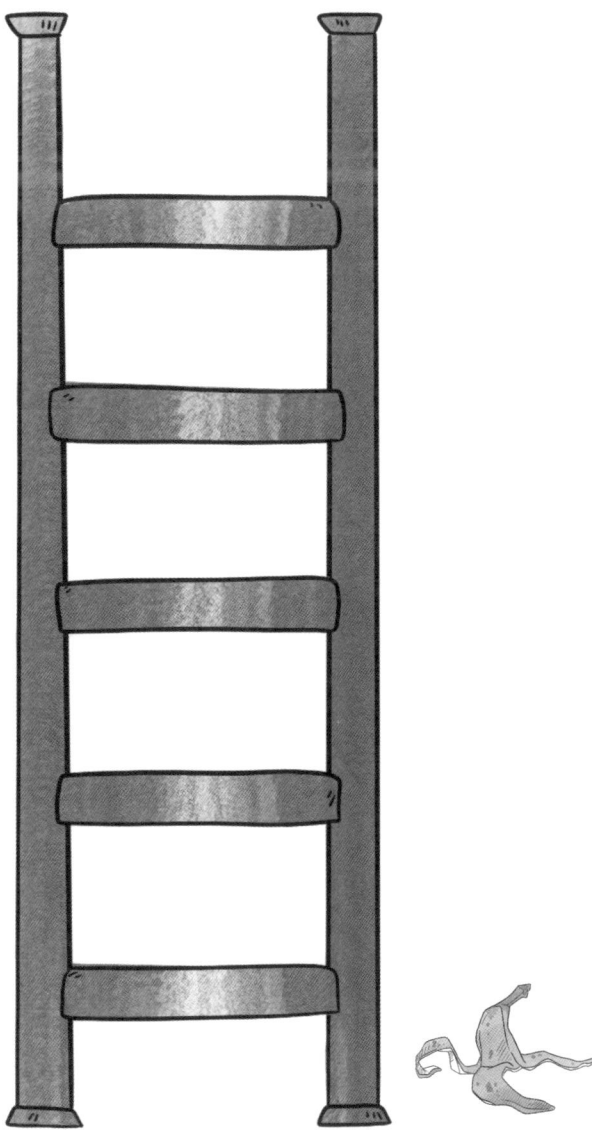

Banana skins are often hard to spot and can be things like:
thinking you're not good enough, anxiety, loss, drugs and alcohol, difficult friendships, missing family, online learning not having the resources you need...the list goes on and on!

The best way to overcome banana skins is learning how to spot them! There is no point ignoring them – you need to deal with them first.

Overcoming Barriers (Part 2)

Think about the types of banana skins you face at the moment. Try writing some down here.

When you are dealing with banana skins – think **STAR**

Stop (and take a deep breath)

Think (about choices you have)

Anticipate (the consequences)

Respond (with the best choice)

Overcoming Barriers (Part 3)

Now look back over your banana skins on the previous page and go through the STAR process. A common example at this time could be…

> I am struggling to complete my school work. I find some of it difficult but don't know who to ask. I can't get motivated to even start and that makes me anxious.

Pretend you are in this person's dream team (Resource 5.5), how would you help them?

So first of all **STOP** and take a deep breath.

Then think about their choices, what could they do?

....

What would the consequences be?

....

How should they respond?

....

If you are not sure of which choice to make – speaking to someone helps, maybe one of your goal keepers or someone else who could help (*even someone just listening can be very helpful*).

Resource 5.5: Creating a Dream Team

Description

Another key characteristic of DYNAMIC goals is to consider not only what the child or young person needs to do but also defining who they may need to support them. Children need a dream team, people around them whom they can turn to for support with their goals. No one does everything on their own, we all need to ask for help sometimes, and it's better that children learn this from an early age. The resources available below are designed to help the adult work with the child on developing their dream team. This includes identifying them first and then elaborating on what specific support they would like from their dream team. Further details on how to use each resource are provided below.

How to use this resource

Part 1: This resource is an information sheet used to introduce the concept of a dream team to the child or young person with whom you're working. It provides some pointers that encourage the child to think about who they would have on their own dream team. It is not meant for completion, but for information only, and to stimulate discussion.

Part 2: This resource can be completed by the child or young person (or by the adult after discussing with the child if the child is not able to do so by themselves). After introducing the concept of the dream team using Part 1, the child or young person has to think of who is around them that they consider to be 'helpers' in achieving their goals. The two kinds of helpers can be described to the child, namely *caring* helpers and *doing* helpers. Some people can be both. The child can be reassured about why this task is important if it's explained that asking for help can be a little scary, so knowing who to ask for the right help can make it easier.

Caring helpers are the kind of people you can talk to, who can give you good advice. They nurture you and your ideas but maybe not the best at doing your hair…

Doing helpers are people who can do things for you, like help you fix your bike or lend you a book. They can offer practical support but are perhaps not who you would go to for a hug.

Part 3: This resource takes the dream team concept to a further level with a worksheet designed to help the child or young person consider specifically how their dream team can support them according to eight key areas: how they can feel safe, healthy, active, nurtured, achieving, respected, responsible and included. By completing this task with the adult, the child can be more specific about the kinds of supports that they would like to have from their dream team, rather than being vague and ambiguous about their roles.

Creating a Dream Team (Part 1)

This is a list of people who can help you to achieve your goals.

Important characteristics of a good dream team are people who…

You see often
At school, home, community (this also includes virtual meetings and telephone calls) and that you trust.

Care about you
And are concerned about your welfare – family, friends, teachers and so on.

You can depend on
They have helped you in the past, maybe they have given good advice or offered a listening ear.

You could help at another time
Help is a two-way street – everyone needs some sometimes, so make sure you help others too!

Creating a Dream Team (Part 2)

We all need a dream team, people around you that you can turn to for support. No one does everything on their own, we all need to ask for help sometimes.

It is important to note that there are two kinds of helpers, *Caring* helpers and *Doing* helpers. Some people can be both. Asking for help can be a little scary, so knowing who to ask for the right help can make it easier.

Caring helpers are the kind of people you can talk to, who can give you good advice. They nurture you and your ideas but maybe not the best at doing your hair…

Doing helpers are people who can do things for you, like help you fix your bike or lend you a book. They can offer practical support but are perhaps not who you would go to for a hug.

Write down the members of your dream team and note what kind of helper you think they are and what they could do to help you. Remember to add at least one person from your school in your team!

Name	Caring	Doing

Do you need to add more members to your dream team?

....
....
....
....

Do you need to add resources to your dream team?

....
....
....
....

Creating a Dream Team (Part 3)

Your dream team care about your wellbeing and want to get things right for you. Wellbeing covers all aspects of your life and can be divided up into key areas, outlined in the boxes below. All together they build up your resilience, basically your ability to bounce back or rebound when things go wrong in life.

Think about, then note down, how things are for you at the moment (under each heading). If things are okay then think about *why they are going well.* If things are not okay then *speak to someone in your team* as soon as possible! To help you think about your answers, have a look at some of the online ideas and supports on our website at www.dynamicassessmentuk.com.

SAFE

Do I feel safe? What makes me feel safe?

HEALTHY

Do I feel healthy? What makes me feel healthy?

ACTIVE

Do I feel active? What do I do to keep active?

NURTURED

Do I feel nurtured (cared for and protected)? What makes me feel nurtured?

We don't have to rely on others to nurture us (although that is important). We can do things to nurture ourselves.

ACHIEVING

Do I feel like I am achieving? What have I achieved?

RESPECTED

Do I feel respected? What makes me feel respected?

Respect should be mutual (it works both ways).

RESPONSIBLE

Do I feel responsible? What am I responsible for?

INCLUDED

Do I feel included? What makes me feel included?

Am I an active member of any groups or local community? Do I include others? How do I feel about my friendships?

Use this space for your ideas and notes…

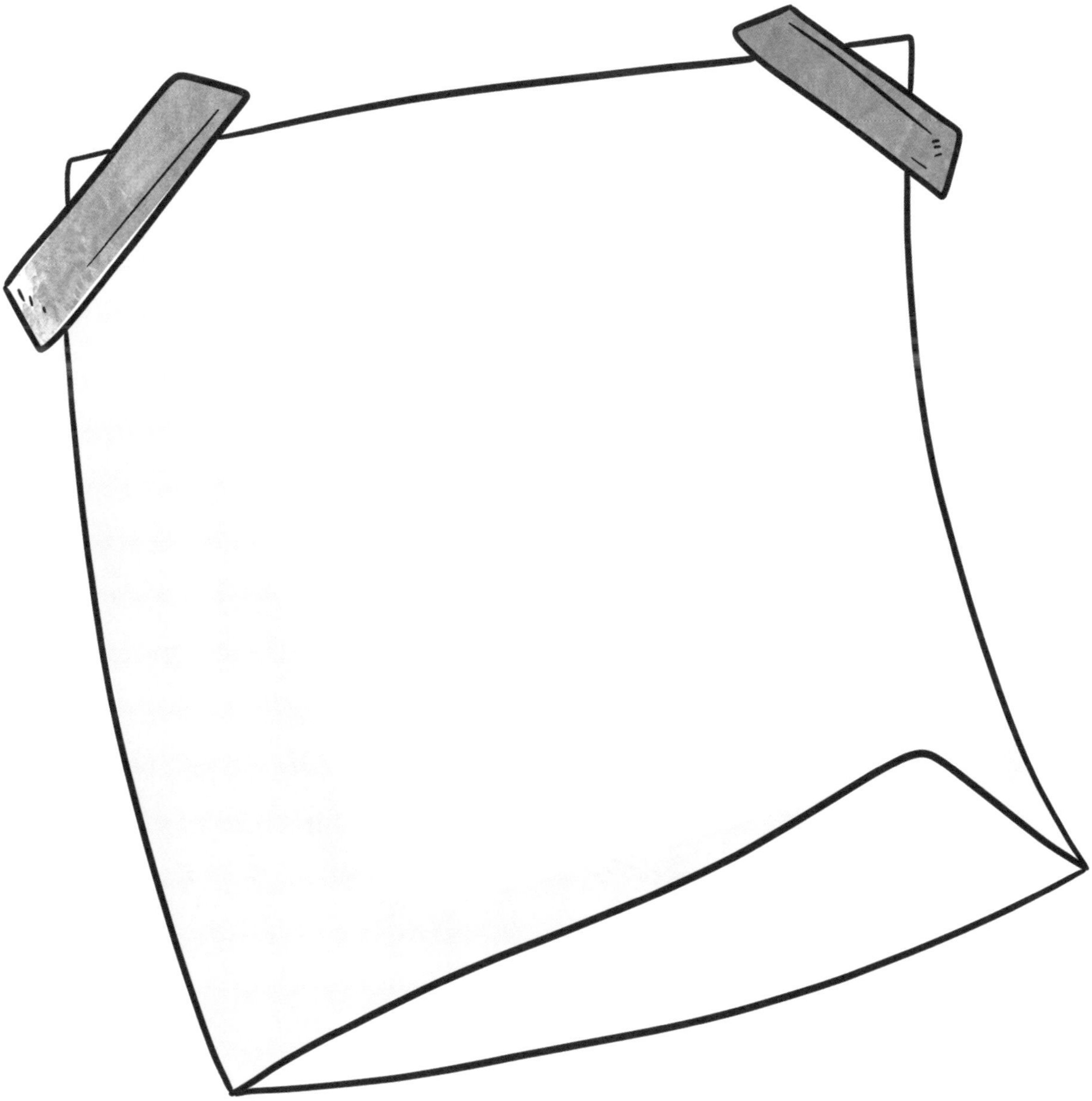

Resource 5.6: Rebounding

Description

This resource focuses on when the child or young person may fall off their Goal Ladder. We rarely achieve our goals first time (plan A), so we need to plan for this. Some people call this preparing for plan B. Instead of giving up, we need to learn how to rebound, like when a footballer hits the crossbar and tries again, or when a spider tries to weave its web but fails and has to start all over again. The worksheet is designed to encourage the child to not give up even if the plan is not working as well as they'd hoped. In other words, it is to reassure the child that it's okay if the plan is not working as well as expected. The important thing is to persevere and understand that they will achieve their goal over time.

How to use this resource

This resource can be used either simply as a stimulus for discussion with the child or young person in circumstances where things are not progressing as well as expected, or in other words, when things are not 'going to plan'. Alternatively, the resource can be used to help the child or young person (with the adult's help) draw up plan B: a new plan, if the original plan hasn't been working effectively. In this resource, the child or young person is reintroduced to the concept of STAR (see Resource 5.4), namely: Stop (and take a deep breath); Think (about choices you have); Anticipate (the consequences); and Respond (with the best choice).

Rebounding

We rarely achieve our goals first time (plan A), so we need to plan for this. Some people call this preparing for plan B. Instead of giving up we need to learn how to rebound, like when a footballer hits the crossbar and tries again.

Are you going to give up if you can't do it first time?

Think back to **STAR.**

If you feel that you are getting off track it can be helpful to think that you are just not there **YET.**

The Power of Yet

I don't get it

I can't do this

This doesn't work

As in

I don't get it…yet

I can't do this…yet

This doesn't work…yet

Think about your rebound plan or plan B. (Remember there are 26 letters in the alphabet, so even if you have to go to plan Z that's fine!)

There'll always be times where we feel we want to give up. Thinking of your goal like a *learning pit* is a helpful way to see the phases we're likely to go through when doing anything different or new.

Resource 5.6 © Fraser Lauchlan and Clare Jones Daly, *Applying Dynamic Assessment in Schools*, 2023

Resource 5.7: Identify Your Own Skills and Strengths

Description
The two worksheets that form part of this resource can be used if children suffer from low self-confidence and need to be reminded of their own skills and strengths. Children with low self-confidence often quickly forget their successes and hold on to their failures. Using this resource can help turn this around so that they will reflect more on their skills and strengths. This will help them to fulfil their goals. The children are asked to consider what their Dream Team think about them (Part 1), and they can write down their own strengths on the worksheet provided (Part 2). The Dynamic Cards (see Chapter 4) can be used to help the child reflect on their own skills and strengths, looking at each of the cards individually to consider which of them would be considered strengths by the child.

How to use this resource

Part 1: This resource can be completed by the child or young person by themselves or with the help of an appropriate adult (especially for younger children or for children with literacy difficulties). They are asked to reflect on a success they have had and then think about the skills and strengths that they displayed that allowed them to achieve that success. This resource also touches on their Dream Team (see Resource 5.5) as children are asked to reflect on what their Dream Team would say about them regarding their positive qualities. It is important for the child to engage in how others can view them positively as too often they will only consider how others will view them negatively.

Part 2: This resource is an extension of Part 1 and takes the analysis of skills and strengths further. It will be more appropriate for older children who will be able to engage in the breakdown of their specific strengths and consider how these strengths will help them reach their goals. It might be helpful for practitioners to use the Cognitive and Affective Learning Principles (child-friendly language) to help the child with completing this resource. The Dynamic Cards, which have graphic representations of the learning principles, could also be used as a means of helping with this more detailed breakdown of the child or young person's strengths.

Identify Your Own Skills and Strengths (Part 1)

A key thing about goal setting is remembering how *awesome* you are!

Identifying your own skills and strengths will help you up the ladder.

Think for a moment about a time you were really proud of yourself. Write about it here.

....
....
....
....

Did you achieve or try something in lockdown or more recently that surprised you?

....
....
....
....

What skills and strengths did you show?

....
....
....
....

What would people in your Dream Team say about you?

....
....
....
....

Sometimes it can be hard to talk about your strengths, but have a go and see if you can find out what your signature strengths are: https://brightandquirky.com/the-24-character-strengths-your-kids-need.

Identify Your Own Skills and Strengths (Part 2)
Use your strengths to support your goals.

Write down a list of your strengths and how these will help you achieve your goals. A couple of examples are provided.

I am good at sticking at things	This will help me to persevere when I find things difficult
I can communicate well with others	I know when and who to ask for help

Resource 5.8: Goal Keepers

Description

This resource is similar to Creating a Dream Team (Resource 5.5). It can be used to assist the child or young person to think about who is important to them, who inspires them. Having a positive role model in your life can boost your motivation to keep going towards your goals when things get difficult, by modelling a guide to success. The child is asked who they admire and why. It could be someone they know well, or not. It could even be someone famous. The child is asked what it is they like about this person, and what traits the inspiring person has that they would like to have themselves.

How to use this resource

This resource may be considered more appropriate for older children in primary and secondary school who are able to engage in the process of reflecting on the characteristics of those people who inspire them. This might be a family member, a friend, somebody famous or perhaps even a member of school staff. The child or young person can complete this resource on their own or with the help of an appropriate adult. They need to think of the traits and personality aspects of their goal keepers and, again, may need help with this from an adult.

Goal Keepers

First, you need to think about who is important to you. Having a positive role model in your life can boost your motivation to keep going towards your goals when things get difficult by modelling a guide to success.

Who do you admire and why? It could be someone you know well, or not. It could even be someone famous. Write a bit about them in the box below, using these questions as prompts:

- What is it you like about them?
- What traits do you see in them that you would like to have? (Are they kind? Strong? Bright? Fun?)
- Do they have the ability to inspire you and others?
- Do they have clear values and vision?
- Are they committed to helping others?
- Are they accepting of others and their goals?
- Do they have the ability to overcome obstacles?

These people can be thought of as *Goal Keepers* – thinking of them can help you to stick to and keep your goals! Reading autobiographies of famous people can often tell you exactly how they achieved their goals.

Resource 5.9: Goal Busters

Description

Goal busters are the opposite of goal keepers. While goal keepers will help you keep your goals, there may well be people in life whose behaviours can cause trouble. We all know someone like this. We say that they are goal busters and will try to make achieving your goals difficult (even if they don't intend to). Sometimes our goal busters are ourselves when we believe (wrongly) that we are not good enough. Sometimes it's our friends who get in the way of our goals and we find it difficult to say no to them. Goal busters are not always obvious, and children may need help to identify them. The intention is that by reflecting on this, children can avoid situations that could harm their goals.

How to use this resource

This resource should only really be used in conjunction with Resource 5.8: Goal Keepers. As with Resource 5.8, it is advised that this resource will be more effective with older aged primary school children and secondary school aged children, since the child or young person has to engage in an analysis of the traits and behavioural aspects of those around them who are goal busters – in other words, those people who can prevent them from achieving their goals, or at least make the achievement of their goals more difficult. Some children may be reluctant to identify their goal busters and may need to be convinced of the benefits of establishing which people (friends, family members, teachers, other adults) in their lives may be undermining their successes, or generally placing obstacles in front of them that prevent them from reaching their goals. Careful support in this task will be required from the adult working with the child or young person.

Goal Busters

While goal keepers will help you keep your goals, there will be people in life whose behaviours can cause trouble. We all know someone like this – they are goal busters and will try to make achieving your goals difficult (even if they don't intend to). Sometimes our goal busters are ourselves when we believe (wrongly) that we are not good enough. Sometimes it's our friends who get in the way of our goals and we find it difficult to say no to them. Goal busters are not always obvious.

Identifying goal busters can help you avoid situations that could harm your goals.

Who are your goal busters? In the box below write some people who could potentially bust your goals.

- Are they often negative about you or your goals?
- Are they often negative about life in general?
- Do they find it difficult to bounce back from obstacles?
- Do they drain your energy?
- Do you find it difficult to say no to them?

Resource 5.10: My Future

Description

If you wish to take the setting of goals further than say a few months or a whole school year, then it can be valuable to help the child reflect on their longer-term goals. Part 1 is a worksheet designed to encourage the child or young person to consider their goals five years from now. The child is asked what they think they might be doing, what they will be like, what they will make them happy, and what their plans are. Part 2 takes this to a deeper level and asks the child or young person to consider any life ambitions they have, and again, in five years' time, to think about breaking down these life ambitions into smaller chunks and reflect on how realistic such goals are.

How to use this resource

Part 1: This resource may be more appropriate for older children in primary and secondary school. As stated above, it is designed for setting longer-term goals and can be a valuable exercise for helping the child or young person understand that what they do *now* can be important for what they do even five years in the future. The child or young person can complete the resource on their own, or preferably in collaboration with a trusted adult. They are asked to consider five specific questions: 1) What do they think they will be doing in five years' time? 2) What will they be like as a person? 3) What will make them happy? 4) What sensations can they perceive (see, hear, taste and feel) around them? 5) What plans do they have?

Part 2: This resource extends the idea of looking into the future and asks the child or young person to consider one overall life ambition, or 'dream', and then break it down into 1) a goal for the next year, 2) a goal for the next five years, and then 3) the overall goal, or life ambition. The child is then asked to consider how realistic it is for them to achieve each of these three goals. The worksheet can be completed in collaboration with an adult who can support them in thinking through how their overall goal can be achieved. Once completed, the worksheet can be taken away by the child and revisited after a year to see if their initial goal is being fulfilled, and if not, why not? Is there a need to reconsider the goals, at least the initial goal of within the year? In this case, Resource 5.6: Rebounding can be useful in formulating revised plans.

My Future (Part 1)
Close your eyes and imagine for a few minutes that it is five years from now.

What will you be doing?

What are you like?

What have you achieved?

What makes you happy?

Let's uncover what you really love. What do you see, taste, hear and feel that brings you joy?

Knowing where you find joy, what are your plans for your future?

My Future (Part 2)

Now on to your dreams.

What would you like to achieve this year, in the next five years or do you have a life ambition?

On a scale of 1–10 how realistic do you think this will be to achieve? Rate each of your goals.

1 ———————————————————————————— 10

1 ———————————————————————————— 10

1 ———————————————————————————— 10

If your goal is big, it is helpful to chunk it/break it down into small steps that you can start now.

For example, if you want to become a *games designer* and that seems so far away in the future, think about your first step… You could *research what you need* to get onto a course, *speak to someone* who has done something similar, *contact someone at school*. The point is that there is *always* something you can do NOW…

And always remember the four key requirements of any successful goal (see Resource 5.3: The Goal Ladder).

Resource 5.11: Visualize Your Goal

Description

This resource has been created to support the child or young person to think of their goals in a different way, by visualizing them. Children can be encouraged by the fact that visualization is a skill that many people (especially athletes) use to see themselves achieving their goals. Some people find it helpful to create a vision board where you can add images and information that inspires you. There are lots of great visualization techniques, and a link is provided in the worksheet to help the child with this.

How to use this resource

This resource will be more suitable with older children of primary age and secondary school age. The child can draw the visualization of their goal on the worksheet themselves, or they can describe it to the adult working with them, who can draw it for them. Alternatively, it may be that the child or young person knows of a talented artist (maybe a friend or family member) who could draw the visualization of their goal for them. The image could be one overall vision, or it could be made up of various different parts. The important thing is that the vision comes from the child or young person, and it is not imposed on them. If the child prefers, or if they are having difficulty with the visualization method, they can write in the box various bits of information that inspires them.

Visualize Your Goal

Visualization is a skill that many people (especially athletes) use to see themselves achieving their goals. Some people find it helpful to create a vision board where you can add images and information that inspires you. There are lots of great visualization techniques online (e.g. https://thejoywithin.org/empowerment-exercises/3-visualization-techniques-for-success-at-any-goal).

How do you visualize your goals?

| Define your goal | Your control | No negativity | Attainable | Measurable | Important to you | Clear and specific |

Resource 6.1: School Ethos for Learning and Assessment

How to use this resource

This evaluation form should be completed by the school leadership team (SLT). The aim is to consider and reflect upon two of the main aspects of the school: school ethos and how formative feedback is used consistently across the establishment. The idea is to assist the SLT to think about how the school can begin the process of change towards becoming a Dynamic School. An initial evaluation is the first step in this process.

School audit

		Yes	No	Unsure	Comments
1.	Our school has a positive ethos				
2.	Assessment is consistent, reliable and transparent				
3.	Assessment is challenging but appropriate				
4.	Assessment outcomes are meaningful and accessible				
5.	Feedback is always given after assessment				
6.	Feedback is always positive and constructive to scaffold progress				
7.	Knowledge and skills are assessed regularly to enhance day-to-day tasks				
8.	Feedback is timely and next steps are clear				
9.	Staff are adopting mediation strategies dependent on learner needs				
10.	Mistakes are welcomed and considered part of learning				
11.	Staff understand the Zone of Proximal Development				

12.	Children understand the Zone of Proximal Development				
13.	We embrace change				
14.	Teachers are confident in using mediation techniques with children				

Any other important aspects of the school that should also be considered?

....

....

....

Resource 6.2: Vision Exercise for Staff

How to use this resource
This exercise should be part of a development session with all staff. Make sure your vision statement reflects your school's aspirations. Keep your vision at the centre of all your strategic decisions; once created, make sure your vision statement is visible to your school community. Think about how you are going to do this. A helpful way to clarify your key message could be in the form of a strapline based on the collective school vision.

A strapline or tagline is a simple one line statement of your purpose or values linked to your collective vision. It portrays the aspirational focus of your school. It should be easily understood by, and have relevance to, all audiences, not just staff; it must be especially clear to children and parents too. What will your school strapline be?

Look at Nike, Apple and Ikea for examples of famous straplines.

Name: ....

Date: ....

| Define your goal | Your control | No negativity | Attainable | Measurable | Important to you | Clear and specific |

Values and Vision Exercise

Clear your mind and close your eyes for a minute or two and think about what your ideal school or class looks like.

Think about a recent time when you were doing your best work.
What were you doing?
What was going on around you?
What values were you showing?

Now consider a more difficult time at work, when you may have been angry or frustrated.
What were you doing?
What was going on around you?
What values were suppressed?

What are your top core values (what is important to you)?
What motivates you?
What do you value in others?

Now create your own personal vision statement, making sure it is DYNAMIC.

....
....

Bullet point three words that sum up your values

- ....
- ....
- ....

Do you want to include these in your strapline? Write your strapline here:

....

Resource 6.2 © Fraser Lauchlan and Clare Jones Daly, *Applying Dynamic Assessment in Schools*, 2023

Resource 6.3: School Readiness Questionnaire

How to use this resource

The 14 questions in this short questionnaire should be answered by all members of the senior leadership team prior to embarking on the project. It allows for any gaps and potential challenges to be identified in order that appropriate planning can be made to mitigate these potential pitfalls before committing to the implementation stage. It can be completed either before or after receiving the completed questionnaires from all staff, but usually will be done before (see Resource 6.4).

School Readiness Questionnaire

Date: ....

Name of school: ....

SLT members (signed): ....

		Yes	No	Unsure	Comments on requirements or date achieved
1.	We are willing to support the process of dynamic change				
2.	We have a basic knowledge of dynamic assessment and the benefits of a dynamic ethos				
3.	Dynamic assessment will be part of our whole school or establishment improvement plan				
4.	We have presented information about the approach to all of our staff				
5.	We recognize the needs and aspirations of our school and believe dynamic assessment to be a good fit				
6.	Opportunities for sharing practice and coaching and mentoring will be provided to embed dynamic assessment				

cont.

		Yes	No	Unsure	Comments on requirements or date achieved
7.	We feel we have the resources required to embed the approach effectively				
8.	We can allocate adequate time effectively for staff to be fully trained in the approach. This may take two to three years				
9.	We will involve parents, carers and children and have suggestions on how we might do this				
10.	We recognize that the Dynamic School is a full school approach and may include partnership agencies and the local community				
11.	We recognize the links with dynamic assessment and other educational theories and key policies already embedded within the school				
12.	We will keep the fidelity of the approach				
13.	We will plan our evaluation prior to commencement of the approach				
14.	We will require additional information before we can take forward the approach				

Resource 6.4: Personal Readiness Questionnaire

How to use this resource

This questionnaire, containing 11 questions, should be completed by all staff working in the school, including ancillary staff. Similar to Resource 6.3, it is essential that this is done prior to embarking on the implementation as it helps to identify needs, gaps and potential challenges. The questionnaire can assess staff receptiveness to the approach and create a shared vision and clarity around expectations and roles (including time and resources). An overarching question here is: Do the values of the new dynamic assessment approach fit with the shared vision of the school? If not, it may be that school staff do not know enough about it and require an introductory session. The readiness questionnaires provide an opportunity to clarify any issues and resolve any tensions before you begin the process. Once all the staff questionnaires are completed, they can be collated alongside the school's senior leadership team's questionnaires (Resource 6.3) and areas of need can be identified.

Personal Readiness Questionnaire

Name (can be completed anonymously) . . . .

Role (e.g. teacher, teaching assistant, janitor). . . . .

Date. . . . .

		Yes	No	Unsure	Comments on requirements or date received or achieved
1.	Our SLT are willing to fully support the model of dynamic change and the dynamic assessment approach				
2.	Dynamic assessment will be part of our school improvement and development plan				
3.	Our senior leadership team have presented information to staff on dynamic assessment				
4.	I have a general understanding of dynamic assessment, its evidence-base and how it can be used within school				
5.	I have or will have opportunities to observe and practise the approach				
6.	I feel that dynamic assessment fits the needs of our school				

7.	I am confident I have the time, skills and resources to effectively implement the dynamic assessment approach				
8.	I feel supported by management, and I am aware of the time and resources I will require				
9.	I am looking forward to working towards being a Dynamic School				
10.	It is important to work with parents and carers on the new approach				
11.	I recognize the importance of coaching and mentoring to embed the approach				

What do I need to help me embed dynamic assessment into my practice?

....

....

....

Resource 6.5: Walk the Walk Planner

How to use this resource

Now you know the underpinning theory of dynamic assessment, you can talk the talk. However, to create real change for learners you need to bridge that theory to practice, or you could say, you now need to walk the walk. The most effective way to walk the walk is to outline the sessions required to embed dynamic assessment and add dates to keep you on track. This questionnaire should be completed by the senior leadership team.

Walk the Walk Planner

Date: ....

Activity	Date	Notes
Dynamic assessment part of school improvement plan		
Audit of school baseline		
Audit of school readiness		
Training/staff session on dynamic assessment mediated learning		
Working party session outline		
Working group 1: Mediation principles Working group 2: Learning principles Working group 3: Stimuli/resources		
Feedback session		

cont.

Activity	Date	Notes
Working group 1: Learning principles Working group 2: Stimuli/resources Working group 3: Mediation principles		
Feedback session		
Working group 1: Stimuli/resources Working group 2: Mediation principles Working group 3: Learning principles		
Final feedback session		
Evaluation		
Feedforward Who will do this? When?		

Resource 6.6: Mediated Learning Principles Group Task

Mediation group

What will you need? Resource 2.2: Checklist of Mediated Learning Principles – Rating Scale, game/activity for one-to-one session video.

The main purpose of this task is for the mediator to reflect on their mediation style and technique while working with a child. It should highlight the mediator's strengths and help them to identify the principles that have the most impact on the child and that they may wish to do more of. Some ideas for carrying this task out: Select a child to observe who either has an individualized learning plan (i.e. GIRFEC or EHCP) or a child you feel would benefit from additional support or exploration of their needs. Video a short one-to-one activity (dynamic assessment type game). A dynamic assessment type of game would be something that the child can try out on their own, then you can mediate and let them try the game again to observe their improved performance (visit www.dynamicassessmentuk.com for some ideas for games and resources to try, or use anything at all that is available in school).

Watch the video back with the mediation checklist and note one or two Mediated Learning Principles. You will need Resource 2.2.

Focus on you, not the child. Bring clips or a four- to five-minute video to share at the next group session.

Questions:

- Was the task suitable?
- How did you find using the video?
- Which mediation principles did you use the most?
- Which mediation principles did you use the least?
- Which mediation principles were the most useful for the child, that had the most impact?
- Any other reflections?

Resource 6.7: Learning Principles Group Task

Learning principles group

What will you need? Additional support needs assistants (ASNAs), Resources 3.1 and 3.2: checklists of Cognitive and Affective Learning Principles.

The focus of this activity is to consider the child's learning ability in each of the areas listed in the checklists of Cognitive and Affective Learning Principles. Were they able to complete the task without help? If they required help and then improved their performance, which areas of the checklists showed this improvement? Some ideas: Select a child working with an ASNA. Use the tick communication box to evaluate the child's progress on tasks, or if you are taking the child out of the clasroom, evaluate how they did with you.

You will need Resources 3.1 and 3.2.

Questions:

- How feasible was it to complete the checklists?
- What task did you use it for – did you focus more on cognitive or affective?
- What did you do if the child completed the task independently?
- What did you do if they needed support over a few attempts (days)?
- Any other reflections? Logistics? Implementation?

Level of interaction checklist:

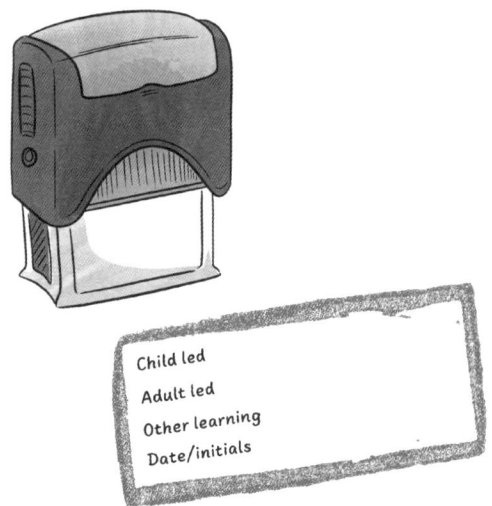

Level of interaction key:

Child led (child can complete task independently with little prompting)

Adult led (child can do most of the task with support/scaffolding)

Learning taking place (child required additional support to stay on task, regulate, etc.)

Resource 6.8: Stimuli/Resources Group Tasks

Stimuli/Resources group

When considering the task or stimuli, you need to balance the fine line of task complexity. The task should be easy enough for the child to experience some degree of success quickly and allow for an appropriate level of challenge. For some ideas and resources, check out the list of easy-to find resources for dynamic assessment at www.dynamicassessmentuk.com.

For this task, try not to think too much about the child's ability or your mediation style (although they will obviously have an impact on how the child engages). Spend the time trying out the cards with the child and discussing their thoughts and understanding of each one, and how they may relate to them. The purpose of this task is for the child to feel confident about their abilities and identify their own strengths as a learner. Encourage the child to offer examples of each of the cards, demonstrating each learning principle or key concept. An example might be: 'I am in my zone when… I dance. I love to dance, I love going to my dance class on a Saturday/I feel happy and relaxed.'

What will you need? 'I am Dynamic' cards, Cognitive and Affective Learning Principles Checklists (Resources 3.1 and 3.2), Mediated Learning Principles Checklist (Resource 2.1).

Select a child in your class with an individualized learning plan (GIRFEC or EHCP) or who could potentially have an individualized learning plan or similar and use the dynamic assessment cards to break down their targets into Cognitive or Affective Learning Principles.
Discuss these using the cards with the child.

Questions:

- How easy/difficult was it to discuss the concepts on the cards?
- Did the child understand the images on the cards?
- Was it easy/difficult for the children to provide real-life examples of the concepts represented on the cards?
- Would you add any other concepts to the cards?
- How would you use your mediation skills to support the child with their targets? (Mediation principles are also in the cards.)

Resource 6.9: Using Video – Top Ten Tips

1. Charge your iPad or camera. It can be extremely frustrating to complete a fantastic dynamic assessment session only to find your camera ran out of battery a few minutes in.
2. Check the audio (having a microphone will help pick up sound better), and make sure the camera picture isn't fuzzy.
3. Avoid shaky footage; use a stand, tripod or prop to hold up the camera rather than someone holding it for you.
4. Choose a good editing program. Good editing software can help turn raw footage into clear, focused clips. iMovie is a great starter program, and more professional options include Adobe Premier Pro.

    The program needs to enable you to:
    - trim and crop videos
    - add text to the video (easier to identify learning principles when labelled)
    - share to your data encrypted files.
5. Keep editing simple.
6. Ask permissions. Ask for your local authority template for video use and GDPR and data sharing.
7. Learn to clip and keep it short. Focus the clips to your objectives, for example demonstrate explicit help from the mediator. When clipping, it can be easier to work from the end time rather than the start time of each clip as the start times will change when you cut the clips.
8. Make sure you can see yourself (if you are observing mediation principles) or the learner (if focusing on learning principles); preferably both should be on camera to record the interaction between both participants.
9. Only focus on one thing when filming, either mediation, learning or task. You can watch the video back afterwards and focus on another area.
10. Feed back video clips to the child you are working with and make sure you use (and clip) child-friendly, positive language.

Resource 6.10: Evaluation: Critical Incident Questionnaire (adapted from the Critical Incident Questionnaire, Brookfield, 1996)

Please take about five minutes to respond to the questions below about the GOALS sessions in class. Don't put your name on the form – your responses are anonymous. Thanks for taking the time to do this. What you write will help us make the sessions more responsive in the future.

Date:

1. At what point in the sessions did you feel most engaged with what was happening?

   ....
   ....
   ....
   ....
   ....

2. At what point in the sessions were you most distanced from what was happening?

   ....
   ....
   ....
   ....
   ....

3. Was there an action that anyone did during the sessions which you found most helpful?

   ....
   ....
   ....
   ....
   ....

4. Did anything happen during the sessions that was confusing or puzzling?

   ....
   ....
   ....
   ....
   ....

5. What surprised you most about the interaction/session? (This could be something that someone else did, or anything else.)

   ....
   ....
   ....
   ....
   ....

6. What will you do/have you done to work more dynamically?

   ....
   ....
   ....
   ....
   ....

References

Austin, J.T. & Vancouver, J.B. (1996). Goal constructs in psychology: Structure, process and content. *Psychological Bulletin*, 3, 338–375.

Beale, S.J. & Crocket, L.J. (2013). Adolescents' occupational and educational goals: A test of reciprocal relations. *Journal of Applied Developmental Psychology*, 34, 219–229.

Bosanquet, P., Radford, J. & Webster, R. (2021). *The Teaching Assistant's Guide to Effective Interaction: How to Maximise Your Practice* (second edition). London: Routledge.

Bosma, T., Stevenson, C.E. & Resing, W.C.M. (2017). Differences in need for instruction: Dynamic testing in children with arithmetic difficulties. *Journal of Education and Training Studies*, 5(6), 132–145.

Bozic, N. (2013). Developing a strength-based approach to educational psychology practice: A multiple case study. *Educational and Child Psychology*, 30(4), 18–29.

Brookfield, S. (1996). Experiential pedagogy: Grounding teaching in students' learning. *Journal of Experiential Education*, 19(2), 62–68.

Bruner, J. (1977). Early Social Interaction and Language Interaction. In H.R. Schaffer (ed.), *Studies in Mother-Infant Interaction*. New York, NY: Academic Press.

Bruner, J. (1995). From Joint Attention to the Meeting of Minds. In C. Moore & P.J. Dunham (eds), *Joint Attention: Its Origins and Role in Development*. New York, NY: Lawrence Erlbaum.

Bruner, J. & Haste, H. (eds) (1987). *Making Sense: The Child's Construction of the World*. London: Methuen.

Callicott, K., Towers, K. & Limniotis, M. (2020). Dynamic assessment: Supporting educational psychologists' practice through the use of video during supervision. *Educational Psychology in Practice*, 36(1), 69–77.

Camilleri, B., Hasson, N. & Dodd, B. (2014). Dynamic assessment of bilingual children's language at the point of referral. *Educational & Child Psychology*, 31(2), 57–72.

Chan, E., Chen, C., Greenberger, E., Dooley, D. & Heckhausen, J. (2006). What do they want in life? The goals of a multi-ethnic, multi-generational sample of high school seniors. *Journal of Youth & Adolescence*, 35, 321–332.

Chaparro, R., Nese, N.T. & McIntosh, K. (2015). Examples of engaging instruction to increase equity in education. *Positive Behavioral Interventions & Supports*, September 2015, 1–14.

Clark, A. (2008). *Supersizing the Mind: Embodiment, Action, and Cognitive Extension*. New York, NY: Oxford University Press.

Danish, S.J. (2002). *Going for the Goal: Leader Manual and Student Activity Book* (fourth edition). Richmond, VA: Life Skills Center, Virginia Commonwealth University.

Deutsch, R. & Reynolds, Y. (2000). The use of dynamic assessment by educational psychologists in the UK. *Educational Psychology in Practice*, 16(3), 311–331.

Dewey, J. (1938). Experience and education. *American Sociological Review*, 3, 917.

Diamond, A. (2013). Executive functions. *Annual Review of Psychology*, 64, 135–168.

Donaldson, M. (1978). *Children's Minds*. London: Croom Helm.

Dweck, C.S. (2006). *Mindset: The New Psychology of Success*. New York, NY: Random House.

Elliott, J. (2003). Dynamic assessment in educational settings: Realising potential. *Educational Review*, 55(1), 15–32.

Feuerstein, R., Feuerstein, R.S., Falik, L.H. & Rand, Y. (2002). *The Dynamic Assessment of Cognitive Modifiability*. Jerusalem, Israel: International Center for the Enhancement of Learning Potential.

Feuerstein, R., Rand, Y. & Hoffman, M.B. (1979). *The Dynamic Assessment of Retarded Performance: The Learning Potential Assessment Device. Theory, Instruments and Techniques*. Baltimore, MD: University Park Press.

Feuerstein, R., Rand, Y. & Rynders, J.E. (1988). *Don't Accept Me As I Am: Helping 'Retarded' People to Excel*. New York, NY: Plenum Press.

Fixsen, D., Blase, K., Metz, A. & Van Dyke, M. (2015). Implementation Science. In J. Wright (ed.), *International Encyclopedia of the Social & Behavioral Sciences* (second edition). Boston, MA: Elsevier.

Flavell, J.H. (1976). Metacognitive Aspects of Problem Solving. In L.B. Resnick (ed.), *The Nature of Intelligence*. Hillsdale, NJ: Lawrence Erlbaum Associates.

Frisby, C.L. & Braden, J.P. (1992). Feuerstein's dynamic assessment approach: A semantic, logical and empirical critique. *Journal of Special Education*, 26(3), 281–301.

Green, J., Liem, G.A.D., Martin, A.J., Colmar, S., Marsh, H.W. & McInerney, D.M. (2012). Academic motivation, self-concept, engagement, and performance in high school: Key processes from a longitudinal perspective. *Journal of Adolescence*, 35, 1111–1122.

Green, R. & Birch, S. (2019). Ensuring quality in EPs' use of dynamic assessment: A Delphi study. *Educational Psychology in Practice*, 35(1), 82–98.

Grigorenko, E.L. (2009). Dynamic assessment and response to intervention: Two sides of one coin. *Journal of Learning Disabilities*, 42(2), 111–132.

Guthke, J., Beckmann, J.F. & Dobat, H. (1997). Dynamic testing – problems, uses, trends and evidence of validity. *Educational and Child Psychology*, 14(4), 17–32.

Hasson, N. & Joffe, V. (2007). The case for dynamic assessment in speech and language therapy. *Child Language Teaching and Therapy*, 23(1), 9–25.

Hattie, J. (1999). Influences on Student Learning. Inaugural Lecture: Professor of Education University of Auckland, 2 August 1999. Available online at www.researchgate.net/publication/237248564_Influences_on_Student_Learning.

Hattie, J. (2012). *Visible Learning for Teachers*. New York, NY & London: Routledge.

Hattie, J. & Timperley, H. (2007). The power of feedback. *Review of Educational Research*, 77(1), 81-112.

Hessels, M. (2000). The Learning Potential Test for Ethnic Minorities (LEM): A Tool for Standardized Assessment of Children in Kindergarten and the First Years of Primary School. In C.S. Lidz & J.G. Elliott (eds), *Dynamic Assessment: Prevailing Models and Applications*. New York, NY: Elsevier.

Hessels, M., Vanderlinden, K. & Rojas, H. (2011). Training effects in dynamic assessment: A pilot study of eye movement as indicator of problem-solving behaviour before and after training. *Educational and Child Psychology*, 28(2), 101-113.

Hill, J. (2015). How useful is dynamic assessment as an approach to service delivery within educational psychology? *Educational Psychology in Practice*, 31(2), 127-136.

Hofer, J. & Chasiotis, A. (2003). Congruence of life goals and implicit motives as predictors of life satisfaction: Cross-cultural implications of a study of Zambian male adolescents. *Motivation and Emotion*, 27, 251-272.

Jackson, L.A., Zhao, Y., Witt, E.A., Fitzgerald, H.E., von Eye, A. & Harold, R. (2009). Self-concept, self-esteem, gender, race and information technology use. *Cyber Psychology & Behavior*, 12, 437-440.

Kozulin, A. (2011). Learning potential and cognitive modifiability. *Assessment in Education: Principles, Policy & Practice*, 18(2), 169-181.

Lauchlan, F. (2001). Addressing the social, cognitive and emotional needs of children: The case for dynamic assessment. *Educational and Child Psychology*, 18(4), 4-18.

Lauchlan, F. (2012). Improving learning through dynamic assessment. *Australian Educational and Developmental Psychologist*, 29(2), 95-106.

Lauchlan, F. (2013). I Think That I Think I Know What I'm Doing: Improving Learning Through the Use of Meta-cognition. In C. Boyle (ed.), *Student Learning: Improving Practice*. Hauppage, NY: Nova Science Publishers.

Lauchlan, F. & Carrigan, D. (2013). *Improving Learning Through Dynamic Assessment: A Practical Classroom Resource*. London: Jessica Kingsley Publishers.

Lauchlan, F., Carrigan, D. & Daly, C. (2007). Bridging the gap between theory and practice in dynamic assessment: A case study. *Educational Psychology in Scotland*, 9(1), 12-18.

Lauchlan, F. & Elliott, J. (1997). Using dynamic assessment materials as a tool for providing cognitive intervention to children with complex learning difficulties. *Educational and Child Psychology*, 14(4), 137-148.

Lauchlan, F. & Elliott, J. (2001). The psychological assessment of learning potential. *British Journal of Educational Psychology*, 71, 647-665.

Leontiev, A.N. (1977). Personal communication cited in Bronfenbrenner, U. (1977). Toward an experimental ecology of human development. *American Psychologist*, 32(7), 513-531.

Lidz, C.S. (2014). Leaning toward a consensus about dynamic assessment. Can we? Do we want to? *Journal of Cognitive Education and Psychology*, 13(3), 292-307.

Litalien, D., Ludke, O., Parker, P. & Trautwein, U. (2013). Different pathways, same effects: Autonomous goal regulation is associated with subjective well-being during the post-school transition. *Motivation & Emotion*, 37, 444-456.

Locke, E.A. (2005). Why emotional intelligence is an invalid concept. *Journal of Organizational Behaviour*, 26(4), 425-431.

Locke, E.A. & Latham, G.P. (2002). Building a practically useful theory of goal setting and task performance. *The American Psychologist*, 57, 705-717.

Maehr, M.L. (1984). Meaning and Motivation: Toward a Theory of Personal Investment. In R. Ames & C. Ames (eds), *Research Motivation in Education*. Orlando, FL: Academic Press.

Massey, E.K., Gebhart, W.A. & Garneck, N. (2008). Adolescent goal content and pursuit: A review of the literature from the past 16 years. *Developmental Review*, 28, 421-460.

Merghati, S.V. & Ahangari, S. (2015). Dynamic assessment of pragmatics: The impact of dynamic assessment on EFL learners' interlanguage pragmatic development. *Basic Research Journal of Education Research and Review*, 1(4), 13-21.

Messersmith, E.E. & Schulenberg, J.E. (2010). Goal attainment, goal striving, and well-being during the transition to adulthood: a ten-year U.S. national longitudinal study. *New Directions for Child and Adolescent Development*, 130, 27-40.

Miser, W.F. (2012). *Giving Effective Feedback*. Available online at www.yumpu.com/en/document/read/53938218/giving-effective-feedback-w-fred-miser-md-the-r-scope.

Naglieri, J. (2000). Intelligence testing in the 21st century: A look at the past and suggestions for the future. *Educational and Child Psychology*, 17(3), 6-18.

Naglieri, J. & Goldstein, S. (2013). *Comprehensive Executive Functioning Inventory Technical Manual*. Toronto, Canada: Multi-Health Systems.

Noble, T. & McGrath, H. (2008). The positive educational practices framework: A tool for facilitating the work of educational psychologists in promoting pupil wellbeing. *Educational and Child Psychology*, 25(2), 119-134.

Nottingham, J. (2007) The Learning Pit. In J. Nottingham (2021), *The Learning Pit*. (n.p.).

Poehner, M.E. & Lantolf, J.P. (2005). Dynamic assessment in the language classroom. *Language Teaching Research*, 9(3), 233-265.

Pribram, K.H. (1973). The Primate Frontal Cortex: Executive of the Brain. In K.H. Pribram & A.R. Luria, *Psychophysiology of the Frontal Lobes*. New York, NY: Academic Press.

Ratner, H., George, E. & Iveson, C. (2012). *Solution Focused Brief Therapy: 100 Key Points and Techniques*. London: Routledge.

Reynolds, C.R. & Horton, A.M. (2006). *Test of Verbal Conceptualization and Fluency*. Austin, TX: Pro-Ed.

Rogers, E.M. (1962). *Diffusion of Innovations*. New York, NY: Free Press.

Seligman, M.E.P. & Csikszentmihalyi, M. (2000). Positive psychology: An introduction. *American Psychologist*, 55(1), 5-14.

Seligman, M.E.P., Steen, T.A., Park, N. & Peterson, C. (2005). Positive psychology progress: Empirical validation of interventions. *American Psychologist*, 60(5), 410-421.

Senko, C. & Harackiewicz, J.M. (2005). Regulation of achievement goals: The role of competence feedback. *Journal of Educational Psychology*, 97(3), 320-336.

Stringer, P. (2018). Dynamic assessment in educational settings: Is potential ever realised? *Educational Review*, 70(1), 18-30.

Tzuriel, D. (1992). *Children's Inferential Thinking Modifiability Test (CITM)*. Ramat Gan: Bar-Ilan University.

Tzuriel, D. (1993). *Children's Seriational Thinking Modifiability Test (CSTM)*. Ramat Gan: Bar-Ilan University.

Tzuriel, D. (1995). *The Cognitive Modifiability Battery: Assessment and Intervention*. Ramat Gan: Bar-Ilan University.

Tzuriel, D. (1999). The Seria-Think Instrument. Ramat Gan: Bar-Ilan University.

Tzuriel, D. (2011). Revealing the effects of cognitive education programmes through dynamic assessment. *Assessment in Education: Principles, Policy & Practice*, 18(2), 113-131.

Tzuriel, D. & Galinka, E. (2002). The Children's Conceptual and Perceptual Analogical Modifiability Test (CCPAM). Ramat Gan: Bar-Ilan University.

Tzuriel, D. & Klein, P.S. (1985). Children's Analogical Thinking Modifiability Test (CATM). Ramat Gan: Bar-Ilan University.

Tzuriel, D., Samuels, M. & Feuerstein, R. (1988). Non-Intellective Factors in Dynamic Assessment. In R.M. Gupta & P. Coxhead (eds), *Cultural Diversity and Learning Efficiency: Recent Developments in Assessment*. Basingstoke: Macmillan.

Vasalampi, K., Salmela-aro, K. & Nurmi, J.E. (2010). Education-related goal appraisals and self-esteem during the transition to secondary education: A longitudinal study. *International Journal of Behavioural Development*, 34(6), 481-490.

Vygotsky, L.S. (1978). *Mind in Society: The Development of Higher Psychological Processes*. Edited by M. Cole, V. John-Steiner, S. Scribner & E. Souberman. Cambridge, MA: Harvard University Press.

Vygotsky, L.S. (1986). *Thought and Language*. Edited by A. Kozulin. Cambridge, MA: The MIT Press.

Wood, D., Bruner, J.S. & Ross, G. (1976). The role of tutoring in problem solving. *Journal of Child Psychology and Psychiatry*, 17, 89-100.

Yang, W., Liu, H., Chen, N., Xu, P. & Lin, X. (2020). Is early spatial skills training effective? A meta-analysis. *Frontiers in Psychology*, 11.

Yeager, D.S., Bundick, M.J. & Johnstone, R. (2012). The role of future work goals in motives in adolescent identity development: A longitudinal mixed-methods investigation. *Contemporary Educational Psychology*, 37, 206-217.

Subject Index

accessible to assistance
   and Affective Learning Principles 36
Affective Learning Principles
   and Can You Colour? 100
   checklist for 85-7
   description of 32, 36-9
   and dynamic assessment materials 43
   and Find Your Way Map 119
   and Learning Principles Group Task 170
   and Learning Profile 48-9
   and Memory Challenge 96
   and Picture Sequencing 104
   rating scale for (adult version) 90-1
   rating scale for (child-friendly version) 94-5
   and Word Bingo 114
assessments
   impact in dynamic schools 64-5
   and Walk the Walk Planner 166-8
   whole school 55-6
attention
   and Affective Learning Principles 37

bridging
   breakdown of 27
   as component of mediated learning 18
   in Mediated Learning Principles practice 23
Bruner, Jerome 17, 18

Can You Colour?
   as dynamic assessment materials task 43
   resources for 100-3
challenging
   as component of mediated learning 19
   in Mediated Learning Principles practice 26
change
   as component of mediated learning 19
   in Mediated Learning Principles practice 26
checklists
   for Affective Learning Principles 85-7
   for Cognitive Learning Principles 82-4
   for Mediated Learning Principles 71-5
Children's Analogical Thinking
   Modifiability test (CATM) 42
Children's Conceptual and Perceptual
   Analogical Modifiability test (CCPAM) 42
Children's Inferential Thinking
   Modifiability test (CITM) 42
Children's Seriational Thinking
   Modifiability test (CSTM) 42

Cognitive Learning Principles
   and Can You Colour? 100
   checklist for 82-4
   description of 29-32, 33-6
   and dynamic assessment materials 43
   and Find Your Way Map 119
   and Learning Principles Group Task 170
   and Learning Profile 48-9
   and Memory Challenge 96
   and Picture Sequencing 104
   rating scale for (adult version) 88-9
   rating scale for (child-friendly version) 92-3
   and Word Bingo 114
Cognitive Modifiability Battery (CMB) 42
cognitive skills
   as component of dynamic assessment 15
collaboration
   as component of dynamic assessment 14
communication
   and Cognitive Learning Principles 33
comparative behaviour
   and Cognitive Learning Principles 33
Comprehensive Executive Functioning
   Inventory (CEFI) 30
concentration
   and Affective Learning Principles 37
confidence in correct responses
   and Affective Learning Principles 37
core features of dynamic assessment 14-15
Creating a Dream Team 134-9
critical incident techniques 65

Donaldson, Margaret 17, 18
dynamic assessment
   core features of 14-15
   description of 13-14
   practitioner practice of 15-16
   staged process of 16
Dynamic Assessment of Cognitive Modifiability, The (Feuerstein et al.) 18
dynamic assessment materials 4-16
DYNAMIC goals 51-2
dynamic schools
   application of dynamic theory 64
   child- and adult-led learning 67-8
   ethos in 56-7
   impact assessments 64-5
   implementation phases 56-68
   implementation science approach 57

dynamic schools *cont.*
   momentum in 65-6
   and Personal Readiness Questionnaire 163-5
   practitioner knowledge and competence 60-4
   and School Ethos for Learning
      and Assessment 155-7
   and School Readiness Questionnaire 160-2
   and school vision 58-9
   and Vision Exercise for Staff 158-9
   whole-school assessments 55-6
Dynamic Triad of Effective Learning 14

Education Endowment Foundation
   (EEF) scaffolding 67-8
efficiency
   and Cognitive Learning Principles 33
encouraging
   as component of mediated learning 19
   in Mediated Learning Principles practice 23
engaging
   as component of mediated learning 18
   in Mediated Learning Principles practice 23
Evaluation: Critical Incident Questionnaire 173-4
executive functioning 30-1
experiential learning 61
explaining
   as component of mediated learning 19
   in Mediated Learning Principles practice 25
exploratory behaviour
   and Cognitive Learning Principles 33
explicit help
   in Mediated Learning Principles practice 22

feedforward
   background to 47-8
   and goal setting 50-2
   and Learning Profile 48-50
   rationale for 47-8
Feuerstein, Reuven
   and Cognitive and Affective
      Learning Principles 30, 31
   and mediated learning 18, 27, 28
Find Your Way Map
   as dynamic assessment materials task 44
   resources for 119-20
flexibility
   and Affective Learning Principles 37
   as component of dynamic assessment 14-15
frustration tolerance
   and Affective Learning Principles 37

Goal Busters 147-8
Goal Ladder 125-30
Goal Keepers 145-6
goal setting
   and Creating a Dream Team 134-9
   DYNAMIC goals 51-2
   and feedforward 50-2
   and Goal Busters 147-8
   and Goal Ladder 125-30
   and Goal Keepers 145-6
   and Identify Your Own Sills
      and Strengths 142-4
   and My Future 149-52

   and Overcoming Barriers 131-3
   and Rebounding 140-1
   and Visualize Your Goal 153-5

I am Dynamic Cards
   as dynamic assessment materials task 44-5
Identify Your Own Sills and Strengths 142-4
implementation phases for
   dynamic schools 56-68
implementation science approach 57
implicit help
   in Mediated Learning Principles practice 22
*Improving Learning Through Dynamic
   Assessment: A Practical Classroom Resource*
   (Lauchlan & Carrigan) 13, 16, 31, 43
independence
   as component of mediated learning 19
   in Mediated Learning Principles practice 24

justification of response
   and Cognitive Learning Principles 34

learning pit 63
Learning Principles Group Task 170
Learning Profile
   and feedforward 48-50
   resources for 121-4
Learning Propensity Assessment Device (LPAD)
   41-2
Leontiev, Aleksei 30

making sense
   as component of mediated learning 18
   in Mediated Learning Principles practice 23
mediated learning
   background to 17-18
   example of 19-22
   Feuerstein's components of 18-19, 27
   methods of 26-7
   theory of 17-18
Mediated Learning Principles
   checklist for 71-3
   competency building guide 76-81
   example of 21-2
   and Mediated Learning Principles
      Group Task 169
   practice of 22-6
   rating scale for 74-5
Mediated Learning Principles Group Task 169
memory
   and Cognitive Learning Principles 34
Memory Challenge
   as dynamic assessment materials task 43
   resources for 96-9
metacognition 62
Mindset (Dweck) 63
momentum in dynamic schools 65-6
monitoring
   as component of mediated learning 19
   in Mediated Learning Principles practice 25
motivation
   and Affective Learning Principles 38
My Future 149-52

nature of response
   and Cognitive Learning Principles 34
Nottingham, James 63

Overcoming Barriers 131-3

Personal Readiness Questionnaire 163-5
Piaget, Jean 17
Picture Sequencing
   as dynamic assessment materials task 43-4
   resources for 104-13
planning
   and Cognitive Learning Principles 34
   as component of mediated learning 19
   in Mediated Learning Principles practice 24
positive outlook
   as component of mediated learning 19
   in Mediated Learning Principles practice 26
practice of Mediated Learning Principles 22-6
practitioners
   dynamic school knowledge and
      competence 60-4
   and Personal Readiness Questionnaire 163-5
   practice of dynamic assessment 15-16
   and Vision Exercise for Staff 158-9
presentation
   and Affective Learning Principles 38
problem definition
   and Cognitive Learning Principles 35

rating scales
   for Affective Learning Principles
      (adult version) 90-1
   for Affective Learning Principles
      (child-friendly version) 94-5
   for Cognitive Learning Principles
      (adult version) 88-9
   for Cognitive Learning Principles
      (child-friendly version) 92-3
   for Mediated Learning Principles 74-5
Rebounding 140-1
recognition
   and Cognitive Learning Principles 35

scaffolding
   as component of mediated learning 19
   and Education Endowment Foundation
      (EEF) scaffolding 67-8
   in Mediated Learning Principles practice 25
School Ethos for Learning and Assessment 155-7

School Readiness Questionnaire 160-2
school vision 58-9
self-regulation
   as component of mediated learning 19
   in Mediated Learning Principles practice 24
sharing
   as component of mediated learning 19
   in Mediated Learning Principles practice 24
spatial awareness
   and Cognitive Learning Principles 35
spatial orientation 63
staged process of dynamic assessment 16
Stimuli/Resources Group Tasks 171
structural cognitive modifiability 18

task perseverance
   and Affective Learning Principles 38
teacher judgement 64
Thornlie Primary School (North Lanarkshire) 66
transfer of learning
   and Cognitive Learning Principles 36
Tzuriel, David 42

Using Video – Top Ten Tips 172

verbalizing
   as component of mediated learning 19
   in Mediated Learning Principles practice 25
visible learning theory 60
Vision Exercise for Staff 158-9
Visualize Your Goal 153-5
vitality
   and Affective Learning Principles 38
vocabulary
   and Cognitive Learning Principles 36
Vygotsky, Lev
   and Cognitive and Affective Learning Principles
      29-30
   and mediated learning 17, 28

Walk the Walk Planner 166-8
Word Bingo
   as dynamic assessment materials task 44
   resources for 114-18

Zone of Actual Development 13, 17, 32, 49
Zone of Potential Development 13, 17, 32, 49, 55
Zone of Proximal Development 13, 17,
   19, 30, 32, 42-3, 49, 63, 156-7

Author Index

Ahangari, S. 14
Austin, J.T. 50

Beale, S.J. 50
Beckmann, J.F. 15
Birch, S. 16, 41
Bosanquet, P. 67
Bosma, T. 14
Bozic, N. 31
Braden, J.P. 15
Brookfield, S. 65, 173
Bruner, J. 17
Bundick, M.J. 50

Callicott, K. 16
Camilleri, B. 14
Carrigan, D. 13, 15, 16, 31, 43, 48
Chan, E. 50
Chaparro, R. 47
Chasiotis, A. 50
Clark, A. 31-2
Crocket, L.J. 50
Csikszentmihalyi, M. 31

Daly, C. 15
Danish, S.J. 50
Deutsch, R. 47
Dewey, J. 61
Diamond, A. 30, 31, 61
Dobat, H. 15
Dodd, B. 14
Donaldson, M. 17
Dweck, C. 63

Elliott, J. 15

Feuerstein, R. 15-16, 18, 27, 31, 32, 41, 49
Fixsen, D. 57
Flavell, J.H. 62
Frisby, C. 15

Galinka, E. 42
Garneck, N. 50
Gebhart, W.A. 50
George, E. 31
Goldstein, S. 30
Green, J. 16, 41, 50

Grigorenko, E.L. 15
Guthke, J. 15

Harackiewicz, J.M. 50
Hasson, N. 14
Haste, H. 17
Hattie, J. 47, 48, 60
Hessels, M. 14, 15
Hill, J. 6, 47
Hofer, J. 50
Hoffman, M.B. 18

Iveson, C. 31

Jackson, L.A. 47
Joffe, V. 14
Johnstone, R. 50

Klein, P.S. 42
Kozulin, A. 15

Lantolf, J.P. 15
Latham, G.P. 50
Lauchlan, F. 13, 15, 16, 31, 43, 48
Leontiev, A. 30
Lidz, C.S. 15
Limniotis, M. 16
Litalien, D. 50
Locke, E.A. 50

Maehr, M.L. 50
Massey, E.K. 50
McGrath, ll. 31
McIntosh, K. 47
Merghati, S.V. 14
Messersmith, E.E. 50
Miser, W.F. 47

Naglieri, J. 15, 30
Nese, N.T. 47
Noble, T. 31
Nottingham, J. 63
Nurmi, J.E. 50

Poehner, M.E. 15
Pribram, K.H. 30

183

Rand, Y. 18
Ratner, H. 31
Resing, W. 14
Reynolds, C.R. 47
Rogers, E.M. 66
Rojas, H. 14
Ross, G. 17
Rynders, J.E. 18

Salmela-aro, K. 50
Samuels, M. 32
Schulenberg, J.E. 50
Seligman, M.E.P. 31
Senko, C. 50
Stevenson, C.E. 14
Stringer, P. 14, 15, 16, 47

Timperley, H. 48
Towers, K. 16
Tzuriel, D. 15, 32, 42

Vancouver, J.B. 50
Vanderlinden, K. 14
Vasalampi, K. 50
Vygotsky, L.S. 13, 17, 29, 20, 49

Wood, D. 17

Yang, W. 63
Yeager, D.S. 50